Praise for *Talk Sense*

"The riveting stories in this volume will make you weep—and learn and grow. What more could you ask for as a parent or a leader?"—*Jerome T. Murphy, Harold Howe II Professor of Education and dean emeritus, Harvard Graduate School of Education*

"*Talk Sense* is simply unmatched in the crowded field of books on communication skills; it is invaluable for leaders. Barry Jentz brings the perfect balance of theory and practical examples to this compact work. His thirty-five years of experience in this field allow him to go to the heart of success with difficult conversations—what it takes to set them up and the skills to bring them to amazingly positive outcomes. Stories, skill-scripts, and explanations make it accessible to veteran and novice alike. There's nothing like it." —*Jon Saphier, founder and president, Research for Better Teaching, Inc., and founder and chairman emeritus, Teachers 21*

"Establishing a new $500 million division within a company is not an easy task, especially when the new division's charter is to take over troubled parts of the company and turn them around, then sell them or return them to their original divisions in the company. The new Metal Refining Division's charter in the AMAX Corporation was exactly that. To make the task more challenging, the troubled parts of the company (metal processing facilities) were located in various parts of the country, targeted at different markets, and employed separate manufacturing processes and technologies.

"When I became head of the Metal Refining Division, I read stories from *Talk Sense: Communicating to Lead and Learn* (CLL) and attended the CLL Seminar. I was so impressed that I brought it in-house for our senior executives. At first, it wasn't an easy sell, because some of these executives had considerable experience (thirty years) and had already achieved success in other divisions of the corporation. By the end of the program, enthusiasm for CLL was so high that we extended it to others in all disciplines.

"I have used the CLL program successfully as the head of other businesses. Throughout my career, I have never seen a program have such an immediate and lasting impact as CLL. It provides the participants with a conceptual framework to better understand themselves and others, as well as useful skills for significantly improving overall communication both within the organization and with customers. It is a sound investment."—*Tony La Russo, former president, Metal Refining Operations, AMAX Inc.*

"When your high-priced management consultant tells you "well, everyone is just going to have to act like an adult," watch out! Your critical project is probably about to derail because of people problems that seem so intractable that even the best business thinkers find themselves hoping they can be wished (or ordered) away. For leaders who have found that just telling people to be different than they are rarely helps, Barry Jentz's *Talk Sense: Communicating to Lead and Learn* offers new hope in the shape of a practical guidebook to transformational learning. Change is never easy, but it is possible for those who have been made willing, by courage or desperation, to examine the reflexive assumptions we would most like to keep hidden. With this book, Jentz shows leaders how to begin the journey."—*Mark Ledden, founding director, Kenning Associates*

"Ordering my finance team to work together (my strong suit) wasn't working, so I read stories that appear in *Talk Sense: Communicating to Lead and Learn* (CLL) and turned to the CLL program. Of course, people bitched but, remarkably, everyone came away with a positive attitude. They began making an effort to listen to what others were saying, genuinely taking the time to understand the wants and needs of others. The knowledge that people hear and react differently to the same situation created an awakening that individuals could learn by listening/seeing how people around them see the world. In fact, my staff got reacquainted with the people around them, after working together for over twenty-five years."—*Eric Resker, former vice president/North American controller, Elkem Metals Company*

"It works! What more do you need to know? Looks like voodoo if you haven't done it. Yet it's useful and tough in forcing the light to go on. Wakes you up. Makes you discover your own WAY, as distinct from other people's legitimate WAYS. *Talk Sense: Communicating to Lead and Learn* is nasty, hard, indispensable stuff for successful leadership—learning to see how you're seen and see the same issue from another's very different view. The more you work at it, the more it works for you. It's worked for me at The Durst Organization and Morgan Stanley!"—*Jeff Meaney, vice president of Security, BCP, Corporate Services, TIAA-CREF*

"Senior managers and leaders are often trapped in their own paradigm of communicating "by reflex," unable to effectively hear colleagues and subordinates or give them useful feedback, feedback that can be used immediately to change behavior and project outcomes. While developing a large commercial office building, we utilized the stories in *Talk Sense: Communicating to Lead and Learn* (CLL) along with the related CLL seminar to create an effective team culture across a disparate group of senior managers and leaders from the real estate, design, and construction industries. This was an extremely aggressive project that was completed on time and within budget, in part because the CLL program provoked us to discover our current, by-reflex paradigm for communication, and challenge it successfully by using "reflective" listening and feedback skills to change our face-to-face interactions. Additionally, every member of the team prized their how-to-work-as-a-team learning and carried the skills forward to other transactions and projects."—*John H. Pierce, vice president and regional manager, Caribbean and Latin America, Turner Construction–International LLC*

During an eighteen-year career as director of Employee Development at the Boston Globe, I had the opportunity and means to contract with the "best and brightest" companies in the field of Human Resource Development. Initially, I contracted with a few of these companies and was invariably disappointed when results fell short of expectations. Then, after reading stories that appear in *Talk Sense: Communicating to Lead and Learn* (CLL) and attending the CLL program with my boss, I used it with as many Globe managers and employees as possible every year for eighteen years to provide them with the mind-and-skill set they needed to work together more productively as well as to improve the company's bottom line.—*Robert D. Henderson, former director of Employee Development, The Boston Globe*

TALK SENSE
Communicating to Lead and Learn

Barry Jentz

 Research for Better Teaching, Inc.

Talk Sense: Communicating to Lead and Learn

ISBN 978-1-886822-09-2

Library of Congress Control Number 2006935129

Research for Better Teaching, Inc.
One Acton Place, Acton, MA 01720
978-263-9449
www.rbteach.com

Contents

Preface

The stories that make up this book are a product of over thirty-five years of coaching conversations with leaders, conducted as a part of the organizational consulting work I do through Leadership and Learning Inc. Those conversations took place with managers and executives in businesses as diverse as newspaper publishing, finance, nuclear power, architectural design and construction, real estate development, international management consulting, engineering, and high-tech start-ups, along with associations of doctors, lawyers, and architects. They also included administrators in tens of public school systems, independent schools, higher education and education-related agencies, government and social service agencies, and day care facilities.

The stories also follow from putting thousands of leaders on videotape in leadership seminars. There, they role-play difficult interactions, analyze their performance, and struggle to make sense of the predictable discrepancies revealed between what they think they do and what they actually do. This videotaping methodology had its origin when I first saw my golf swing on videotape. Admittedly, the person swinging the club looked like me, but *my* swing was balanced and smooth, not the spastic lurch I saw on the screen. Flat out, I told the golf pro, "That's not my swing!" "Oh. Okay. I'll tape you again," he replied.

The pro played back the second video; again I opened my mouth to deny the evidence of my own eyes—and then closed it as I finally faced the embarrassing truth that the image in my head was more real to me than the reality on screen. I might never have believed it without viewing the tape.

It turns out that I am not alone in clinging to a discrepancy between what I think I do and what I actually do. Repeatedly, when I put leaders on tape to handle difficult interactions in seminars, they see themselves doing one thing and get feedback that they are doing quite another. Often what follows from the feedback are moments of insight ("I don't listen at all, do I?!") and the motivation to self-correct by practicing new skills.

I fell in love with producing these moments of insight into discrepancies between our self-images and actual practice and with enabling leaders to close the gaps. When they do, their interactions with others result in increased trust and credibility, the bedrock necessary for improving performance. Teamwork and products improve. Profits increase. And at home, marriages come back to life, and parents make new contact with their kids. Families re-form.

The stories that follow in this book are an invitation to take part in a journey from insight to the skillfulness that produces this rich set of outcomes.

Introduction

The manager in charge at a nuclear power plant hears an emergency alarm, alerting him to the threat of a deadly radiation leak. A control operator on the manager's five-member team checks the reactor systems and reports a finding that is the exact opposite of what the manager expected. The manager is stunned.

"Oh, no!" he says to himself, "What's going on?" His operations team stares at him and waits.

All of us hope that the manager is not the type of person who fits the following description, though we all know people like this at work and at home:

> He talks tough and always thinks he is right, even when he doesn't know what's going on, blaming circumstances on other people. To him, the only alternative to in-charge decision making is wishy-washy weakness. He hates uncertainty, so takes action even when his ways of explaining things are inadequate. Feedback is always an attack. Although he only talks and never listens, he claims he does. He has no ability to engage other people in making new sense with him and figuring out what to do in difficult situations.

Such a person could cause a nightmare for all of us because he is defensive, incapable of learning in the sense of making new sense and inventing new behavior through interaction with other people. The situation requires someone who can know he is confused, assert that confusion without shame or pretense, and engage his team in making new sense and inventing actions to avert a disastrous radiation leak. It calls for someone who can make good decisions about how to learn before deciding what to do.

All of us would hope that the nuclear manager fits this contrasting description of a different person:

> He talks sense, asserting himself when he thinks he is right *and* when he doesn't know what's going on or what to do. Confidently, he lays out his confusion and articulates messy situations, inviting his group to present new information, explanations, and feedback that he uses to question his own thinking, as well as theirs. He listens actively, sets out his reasoning, gives immediate feedback, synthesizes, and gets decisions made. Through interaction with him, people learn, change, and grow to be more productive.

This is a description of a person who leads through interpersonal sense making. He is much more likely to avert disaster than the man in the first description because he has confidence even when he is lost and confused, and he

1

has a set of interpersonal learning skills that enable him to make new sense and invent new action with others. By contrast, the first manager's confidence exists only when he has an answer, and he lacks the interpersonal skills to learn with others and act to avert disaster.

As different as these two men are, they are similar in that they must make new sense of unexpected events. As sense makers, they (and we) can be in one of three internal conditions or places. First, they can have sense made, in which case their explanations for things work. Second, if their explanations do not work, as in the incident above, they find themselves suddenly searching for sense, or trying to find alternative explanations and behavior that do work. Third, should their search prove fruitless, they find themselves in "no sense," or stuck. (See Table I.1.)

Table I.1 Internal Conditions for Sense Making		
Sense Made	**Searching for Sense**	**No Sense**
When we have sense made, we can explain why events occur. Our theories, or reasons, or explanations work. Day to day, we are not even aware that we are sense makers until an unexpected event disrupts the sense we have made.	Something happens that disrupts the sense we have made, so we are forced to start searching for new sense. We describe this condition as puzzling, figuring, wondering, exploring, questioning, searching for under-standing, hypothesizing, or trying to put the pieces together.	When our search for sense fails, we often say, "I'm at a loss to make sense of this!" Our internal condition might be called "no sense," and we describe ourselves as confused, lost, stuck, at our wits' end, stymied, up a creek without a paddle, between a rock and a hard place, nonplussed, stumped, baffled, perplexed, shut down, trapped, bewildered, at an impasse, befuddled, or bemused.

Like all of us, the two managers in the example are similar in that they prefer to have sense made of their lives: their confidence is high when they have answers to the questions life poses at work and home. Where they differ significantly is in how they relate to themselves and others when they do not know what is going on, let alone what to do about it.

The first manager is likely to experience his not knowing as a liability, to freeze, and to isolate himself, while the second will use his confusion as a resource in an interaction that produces new sense and behavior.

We need not picture a situation verging on nuclear disaster to recognize the urgent importance in our work lives of developing our capacity for talking sense with each other.

Imagine a newspaper company that controls 70 percent of the advertising revenue for its metropolitan area. The executives have sense made of who they are as a company and of their relationship to their market. Then direct mail advertising arrives, and newspaper ad revenue begins to plummet. The executives scramble to make sense of what is going on as each month more revenue disappears. In this unnerving situation, they wonder, Will this rate of decline continue? Who are those guys? Our biggest advertiser is talking with them. Should we lower our rates? What should we do?

After nearly six months of sense-making turmoil, they decide to buy a direct mail advertising company and are able to recover about half of the lost revenue. As their revenue figures rise, they gradually begin to trust a new sense of who they are now as a company and of their new relationship to the market.

Then three years later, cable TV takes off. Once again, advertising revenues plummet, the executives' sense is lost, and they must search for new sense.

And then comes the Internet.

If the executives in this story cling privately to their sense of how their business worked before direct mail advertising, cable TV, and the Internet, simply defending it against the intrusion of new data, their company is doomed. Their value to the organization is in direct proportion to their ease and resourcefulness as interpersonal sense makers. In interaction with other executives, they must let go of their natural tendency to defend the sense they have made and risk a search for new sense.

A whorl of constantly changing circumstances at work and home calls on us to perform in a new way—as learners capable of making new sense and inventing new behavior in interaction with others. In fact, our lives are increasingly punctuated by "Oh, no!" moments not dissimilar to the ones experienced by the manager at the nuclear plant and the newspaper executives.

At work, how many times in the past year has your usual way of making sense of things been disrupted by:

- A change in boss or team members
- Restructuring, altered roles and responsibilities
- Product or service changes

- Shifts in customer needs

- Personnel issues stemming from diversity issues or legal threats

- Budget and staff cuts or additions prompted by decelerating or accelerating growth

- New competitive threats

- Unexpected career opportunities or disappointments

At home, how many "Oh, no!" moments fractured the sense you had made of yourself in relationship with the key others in your life: your parents, spouse, children, extended family members, friends, neighbors, community members, elected officials?

Amid continual upheaval in our sense making, we are called on to act in difficult situations:

- Parents must respond to a son's announcement that he is dropping out of college during his junior year.

- A corporate owner must relate to an important prospective client whose behavior baffles and even angers him.

- An administrator must coach a new employee who is seen as too pushy.

- An executive must respond to his wife's telling him that if he does not stop treating her like a problem to be solved, she will leave him.

- A new engineering manager is told by her supervisors that her ideas for change will not work.

- A lawyer, doctor, or principal must respond to an angry or confused or unmotivated client, patient, or student.

Ease and resourcefulness as interpersonal sense makers do not come naturally. In fact, when circumstances jolt us with information that shatters our sense of a situation, we feel threatened. Our impulse is to protect our current thinking and hide our consternation from others. While we privately scramble inside, we defend outside in the interpersonal world, communicating to fix the person or situation that disturbed our sense.

In fact, we typically behave more like the first manager in the nuclear power plant than the second manager. When life's uncertainties shake us, we talk tough, or try to, rather than talking sense.

How we can move ourselves and others from a protective or corrective mode of communication to the openness of interpersonal sense making at work and at home? The shift requires personal change. We must develop a set of skills for reflecting on and changing our own thinking and behavior and for enabling others to do the same.

Overview of the Book

This book is designed to accompany you on a reflective journey into the nature of your behavior, including its consequences and antecedents, and to help you envision a new destination.

The structure of the book follows the four phases that make up the journey from communicating to fix to communicating to learn, phases that are at once a sequence and a continuing cycle of change. (See Table I.2.)

Table I.2 **Phases in the Journey** **From Communicating to Fix to Communicating to Learn**
1. **Discovery:** Discovering that we communicate to fix people rather than learn with them
2. **Invention:** Inventing an internal voice that believes in interpersonal learning and is as strong as our fix-it voice
3. **Practice:** Practicing how to embody in behavior our intention to learn
4. **Action:** Acting to learn with others in a fix-it world, so that trust is built, quality is increased, productivity is improved, and people's ability to learn in the future is enhanced

Chapter One invites you to discover gaps between what you think you do when you communicate and what you actually do, on the assumption that you cannot get where you are going unless you know where you are starting from.

After you have located where you are starting from, you need the guidance of a new inner voice to get you to your new destination. Chapter Two shows how to invent and nurture this new voice.

Chapter Three, which looks at practice, is designed to prepare you for the journey by linking your new internal voice with behavior that is congruent with its values and principles.

Action, the topic of Chapter Four, focuses on the application of new ideas and behavior. It pictures in dialogue stories how individuals have struggled to transform typical, difficult interactions into opportunities for learning and change.

Chapter Five provides further guidance in the form of tips, techniques, methods, and explanations to assist and comfort you on your journey. Chapter Six is a conceptual summary. Please do not assume that the book must be read sequentially. You might read the Conceptual Summary first. After reading the Introduction to the book and first story, you might read the stories in the chapter on action before reading the instructional material in the chapter on practice. For only one example, you might read the "Million Dollar Listening" story to answer the questions, Why would I learn these skills? What's the payoff?

This is a book of stories, not a book of lists of, say, the six keys to asserting yourself or the four ways to influence others. In a book of lists, if you lose your bearings, you can always look up and find the equivalent of a green interstate highway sign telling you exactly where you are: point three of the five ways to handle whatever, for example.

Though one seldom gets lost in a book of lists, the knowledge acquired is often informational in nature. But when we face difficult interactions, our emotions crowd out rational thinking. Such knowledge is useless under pressure unless it has been rediscovered through the insight that comes with the attempt to practice and embody it. Insight can be gained from a book of stories through our vicarious participation with the lead characters as they handle difficult interactions.

In allowing ourselves to be drawn into a book of stories emotionally as well as intellectually, we accept the risk that we will at times feel lost and wonder what the point is. If you find yourself in this situation, try going to the Contents of Chapter Six (the Conceptual Summary), the material at the beginning and end of the chapters, or the "how-to" parts of the Practice section in Chapter Five.

I hope that the stories here will both move you and bring you along a journey of personal learning. My aim is to a strike a balance between exposition that gives you easy access to the ideas and narrative that lets you experience them emotionally.

The characters portrayed in the stories in this book are corporate owners, higher education administrators, platoon sergeants, CEOs, accounting supervisors, college students, and managers, as well as husbands, wives, mates, and parents. All are smart, competent, and successful, as well as limited, struggling, and sometimes lost. If you can see yourself in some of these people, perhaps you will reflect on your own behavior and consider the possibilities offered here for making communication an act of interpersonal learning.

The first story, "A Son Drops Out of College," illustrates how, without knowing it, we communicate to fix people rather than communicate to learn together. The story is set in a home context, though it was told in a professional consultation between a woman CEO and an organizational consultant.

Story: A Son Drops Out of College

"What could we have done?" the woman asked an organizational consultant with whom she was meeting in regular coaching sessions. The CEO and owner of a company, this mother of five grown sons was remembering the incident that resulted in the disappearance of her youngest son. His abrupt departure had prompted her to use some of this time to make sense of what had happened.

She had not heard from her son for eight weeks. Never before had she been out of contact with one of her children for so long. For all she knew, he was dead.

He had come home during the second semester of his junior year in college and announced that he had dropped out of school. A series of arguments ensued between the young man and his parents. Each argument, begun civilly, ended in acrimony, with the parents angry and confused and the boy estranged. The mother recoiled as she remembered the disharmony of these exchanges. Yet she felt a strong need to understand what had caused her son to leave.

"He said, 'I study hard, and I know the material. . . . But when I get in there to take the test, I just can't put it down on paper!'"

"That's what he said. I'm sure that's what he said." The woman repeated her son's words verbatim, apparently hoping the sound would satisfy her longing for clarity. That had been the last thing he said to his parents. At their response, he had burst from his chair at their kitchen table, thrown a few things in a carrying bag, and left the house immediately.

What had happened? These parents were not unusually ineffective communicators. The hours of argument with their son prior to his departure were of a form quite typical of all our face-to-face interactions, whether at home or work. All of us communicate in this way: we give information to one another, back and forth, repeatedly. In giving information, we are tacitly asking others to listen to that information. But others do not listen. They give us information back. In giving information back, they are tacitly saying to us: "No, I cannot listen to you. I need you to listen to me."

This pattern of interaction, called *competition for listening*, is outlined in the left column in Table I.3 and illustrated in the right column by an actual exchange between the father and son in this story.

Table I.3 Competition for Listening	
Outline of the Pattern	**Illustrative Dialogue**
1. Initiator: Gives information, tacitly asking the receiver to listen.	Father: There's no future today without a college education.
2. Receiver: Gives information back, tacitly saying, "No, you listen to me."	Son: There are plenty of people who make it. Look at Bill Gates.
3. Initiator: Gives information back, tacitly saying, "No, you listen to me."	Father: That's the exception. You need a college degree.
4. Receiver: Gives information back, tacitly saying, "No, you listen to me."	Son: The exception makes the point, though!
5. Initiator: Gives information back, tacitly saying, "No, you listen to me."	Father: No it doesn't. You're not the next Bill Gates!

The competition-for-listening pattern is the interpersonal form taken by the defensive reactions we all want to believe we don't have. This kind of interaction costs families and organizations countless hours of lost productivity and learning, as well as heartache.

The father, mother, and son in this story conversed for hours in the competition-for-listening pattern. In the two examples that follow, notice how each person tacitly asks to be listened to by giving information, only to receive information in return that says tacitly, "No, I cannot listen to you. I need you to listen to me."

Father: What's the problem? Is the work too hard or boring? The instruction lousy? A girlfriend giving you a bad time? Give me a break here. What's going on?   INQUISITIVE

Son: It's just not working.

Father: I'm calling the dean because this makes no sense! You can't just quit!

Son: It's a done deal.

After fruitless hours of competition-for-listening arguments with their son, the parents often went after one another in the same form:

Husband: You have always been too easy on him. He's never learned to stand on his own feet!

Wife: And you? You do nothing but find fault! It's one string of negatives after another.

Husband: This recrimination gets us nowhere! It's not our fault! He's got to finish school!

Wife: You're going to order him back, again? That's been very successful so far.

Of course, when the son said to his parents, "I study hard, and I know the material. . . . But when I get in there to take the test, I just can't put it down on paper!" he was giving them information, tacitly asking them to listen, but they could not. They gave him information back, tacitly saying, "No, we cannot listen to you; listen to us." The parents' actual words were:

Father: Well, you just can't be studying hard enough!

Mother: I know this is difficult, but you are going to be all right!

Were these parents to face the same moment again with their son, what might they say to increase the likelihood that he would keep contact rather than bolt? Contact keeps hope for relationship alive. Without relationship, there is no learning, no change, no growth through interaction.

The mother continues to meet with the consultant during the son's disappearance, and in one of their meetings, he agrees to meet with the three family members if the son returns, to begin a conversation from the point in the interaction that apparently led the son to flee.

The son does come home, and his mother holds the consultant to his word. The father had previously refused his wife's request to join her for a coaching session, but the mother's relentless assertion results in a plan whereby the consultant meets with the father, then the mother and father, and finally with mother, father, and son together.

The meeting with the father is understandably tense from the outset, even as both men try for small talk and acknowledge that this is a voluntary activity. They agree that as a result of information exchanged in this meeting, either man or both might decide not to go ahead with the subsequent meeting. The consultant reviews:

- His understanding of the goals the parents have for their son. First, they want to raise a son who is confident and capable of making sense of his own life and acting assertively to take care of himself. Second, they want to reestablish contact. Third, they want him to finish his schooling.

- The occasion at which their goals and relationship with their son were ruptured.

- His plan for the four-way meeting, previously discussed with the man's wife, to reset the scene at the kitchen table where the three of them last spoke, ask the son if he remembered speaking the words "I study hard," and then tell the son that his parents want to try to respond differently to him, with the hope of finding a connection where there is estrangement.

The two men then look together at a piece of paper on which are written the son's words followed by what the parents said, as remembered by the mother:

Son: I study hard, and I know the material. . . . But when I get in there to take the test, I just can't put it down on paper!

Father: Well, you just can't be studying hard enough!

Mother: I know this is difficult, but you are going to be all right!

The husband confirms his wife's memory of the interaction and talks about how everything he and his wife have tried in an attempt to get their son to return to college has not worked, reiterating the content and competitive pattern of exchange outlined at the beginning of this story.

The consultant tries to focus them on the son's words, asking, "When your son spoke as he did, what do you think he might have been saying?"

"He's kidding himself about studying hard enough."

"You said this to him, trying to help him come to his senses?"

"Obviously."

"He didn't come to his senses, though. He got up and left?"

"Right."

"So what you're trying to figure out, and you're looking for help from me on this, is how to get your son to stop kidding himself and buckle down to study so he can meet this challenge and succeed?"

"Exactly!"

"I want to help you and your son," the consultant says. "But I think that the two of us are looking at your son's words and seeing them differently. Your son could have a 'kidding himself about studying hard enough' problem, the solution to which would be 'buckling down,' and yet to me, he seems to have a different kind of problem—a 'can't-make-sense problem.' Logically, studying hard and knowing the material should result in doing well on tests, not freezing up. Apparently he can't fit these discrepant pieces together. I'm suggesting that either you or your wife ask your son if he sees himself in this kind of quandary. If he does, then perhaps he'll ask us to join him in figuring out what's going on."

Interrupting, the father explodes at the consultant: "That's preposterous! I won't make my son a weakling! And neither will you or my wife! He is *not* going to wallow in his own nonsense. He's going to pull himself together and prove he can get through school!"

Apparently, in the father's mind, to ask his son if he were in a quandary would be to emasculate him. It would be to invite his son to "wallow in his own nonsense." The father's remedy is to move the young man in the opposite direction, to pull him "out" of the toxic stuff (nonsense) he is "in."

The consultant replies, "You're going to be a voice of strength that your son can count on, unequivocally?"

"That's right," the father responds, glaring.

"And what I'm suggesting would violate your commitment to giving him strength. In fact, to ask him if he is stuck would be to invite him to be weak?"

"Yes!"

The consultant continues, "Logically, that makes sense. At the same time, I don't think your son would receive your inquiry with his logical mind. I think it would reach him in the heart, and he might feel stronger because you can see (and, I hope, accept) him as a person who is lost, rather than . . . "

The father bursts out sarcastically, "You want *both* of us to be cripples!"

"No, I want you to be partners in figuring out what's going on in his life and what might be done."

Just then the mother arrives. The father turns from the consultant and walks toward his wife, motioning with a wave of his hand that she should leave the room with him. They leave. The consultant is unsure whether the father will return and take part in the four-way conversation. He is ambivalent about proceeding himself.

The father returns to the room alone and walks up to the consultant.

"You better know what you're doing!" the father says to the consultant with a quiet but edgy urgency.

"You've decided to give this a try?" the consultant asks. He waits, watching the father for a sign of commitment. The father's face is stone, but he does not walk out.

After several moments of silence, the father says, "It's because of her," apparently referring to his wife.

"You're trapped?" the consultant inquires, knowing that the wife told her husband that she would leave him if he did not participate in this encounter.

Again, the father does not speak, though his lips purse and then open, as if he intends to say something.

"Well, I think you're torn," the consultant says, continuing to focus on the fact that the father is making himself available physically, even though he is not responding verbally. The consultant continues, "This whole thing makes no sense to you. You hate it. At the same time, you want connection with your wife and son, and your efforts have failed, so you need help."

The consultant pauses, expecting an interruption. It does not come. The father never does speak, but his eyes remain available and he makes no move to leave.

The mother enters the room, explaining that she has spoken to the son by phone and expects him momentarily. The consultant invites her and her husband to sit at a small, round table suited for four people, and they do so, across from one another. When the consultant sits, he:

- Restates the differences between himself and the husband about the possible condition of the son at the time he spoke and the nature of an appropriate new way to respond to him

- Gives each of them a new piece of paper with the words he suggests one of them say to their son

- Explains that the words might cause the son to tear up or cry, expressing grief for not feeling heard by them over the years

When the son arrives, the father gets up, barely acknowledging his son with a glance, and then leaves the room. In his absence, the wife introduces the son to the consultant, and they trade small talk as he sits opposite the consultant. When the father returns minutes later, he sits in the chair across from his wife.

After a review of the events leading to this meeting, the consultant outlines his plan for the meeting and hands the son a piece of paper with the words that his mother recalled him speaking immediately before he disappeared.

The son confirms saying these words and agrees, hesitantly, to say them again, offering his parents an opportunity to respond differently. After a long breath and a brief look at the consultant, he reads from the paper: "I study hard, and I know the material . . . " The rote tone in his voice gives way to the emotion of the moment and his still very real dilemma. His voice breaking, he continues: "But when I get in there to take the test . . . I just can't put it down on paper."

The father, his hands trembling slightly, sits in silence staring at the paper in front of him, apparently deciding whether to read the words written there by the consultant. Then, a word at a time, he begins, and as he does, he lifts his eyes to meet those of his son and reads slowly, hesitantly: "You . . . are . . . at . . . a . . . loss . . . to make sense of this situation?" (5)

The son's eyes well up with tears, and the room full of silence gradually admits the muffled, hacking sound of a son who is trying, unsuccessfully, not to weep. Years of grief for not being known by his father insist on squeezing through the son's reluctant throat and eyes.

Like statues too brittle to risk movement, the parents sit frozen, afraid and confused, and waiting for an end to the silence.

When he regains his ability to speak, the son looks at his father without malice and says slowly: "That's the first time in twenty years that you listened to me—to *me*."

He says this because his father's response, however choreographed, did not dishonor him by treating him as a deficiency to be fixed, as if he were in some forbidden or toxic or wrong place his parents had to get him out of by replacing his sense (being at a loss) with their sense (you're kidding yourself about studying hard enough; or, you're going to make it if you try). Quite the contrary, his father's response recognizes him for what he is in: a quandary. The response honors the legitimacy of the son's confused existence at this moment in time, as if saying, "Pull your chair up to this table. I'm proud to talk with a son of mine who is at a loss to make sense of his life. There's no shame in losing sense or in searching for it. You don't have to live alone in that condition. We can talk about your quandary together."

The son's words about being listened to for the first time floor his father. A mixture of disgust and befuddlement comes out as, "What are you talking about?"

"I'm talking about when I don't have my act together. You and mom . . . ," the son's voice trails into a note of hopelessness.

Exasperated, searching, the father at once blurts and bites off the words, "What's the problem, here?"

"We what?" asks the mother.

"It's not you; it's me," the son says, both angry and apologetic as he retreats into self-doubt and shame.

The son's silent response to his parents is interrupted by the consultant, who asks the son, "It's difficult to find the words for what you wanted to express?" (6)

"Yeah," the son says, pausing. Then he continues, "Everything is fine as long as I fit the program. When I don't, you don't want to hear about it. So I don't tell you. This test-taking thing slipped out. I must've been desperate."

"But we want to help you!" the mother says urgently.

(7)

"I know," the son replies, "and that makes it worse." He stares down at the table.

"Their ways of helping leave you in a bind?" asks the consultant.

"Exactly. I know they're trying to help, but I end up feeling like nothing."

"You begin to feel hopeless about ever communicating with your mom and dad when you're 'off the program'?" the consultant asks.

As the tears well up again in the son's eyes, his father's eyes cloud with sadness and confusion. His forehead wrinkles with the apparent strain of wrenching himself to make sense of his son's bewildering responses. Wide-eyed in concern, the mother waits.

"You'd think I'd committed a crime," the son says plaintively, apparently referring to how he feels on the receiving end of interactions with his parents.

"You're left feeling in the wrong, and ungrateful to boot, because you aren't responsive to your parents' help?" asks the consultant.

"Yes," said the son. Looking first at his mom, then his dad, and back at his mom, he begins to speak: "I know . . ." But then he stops and stares into the depths of his own mind.

The silence persists again.

Asked by the consultant if they are confused by their son's responses, both parents agree.

The consultant asks the son if he could help his parents by giving examples of the off-the-program experiences he had learned to hide and describe what each of them did that turned him off. The son articulates that "off the program" refers to those times when he is "mentally fractured," "confused," "uncertain," "scrambled," in "bits and pieces."

Flabbergasted is the word for his parents' reaction to his feeling abandoned by them at these times. With the consultant's help, the son relates his first conscious memory of reaching out to each of them when he was in "bits and pieces" rather than assured.

For his father, the son recalls pitching in a Little League baseball game when he wasn't at his best. Ten pitches, and he knew his body was not his to control on this early evening in May, with parents in professional clothes crowding the baselines, at once eager for their children's success and a quick end to the game, so dinner might be had before eight o'clock.

He walked the first batter, gave up several hits, walked two, gave up a home run and several more hits, another walk, two more home runs—all in all, eleven runs in an interminable, hour-long first half of a first inning with only one out.

The coach, his father, has called time for a conference and walks slowly to the mound. The son waits, standing alone in a desolate lake of humiliating silence. His own team's cries of, "Attaboy, chuck it in there!" have long since ended, and with the calling of time, even the parents' conversations are hushed. Waiting, the son struggles not to drown in a smothering mix of anger, relief, fear, and failure. He will not cry.

When his dad finally arrives, a voice the son recognizes as his own rises unexpectedly and says, "I'm not sure I've got it today."

The coach's eyes and mouth respond emphatically, making his incomprehensible words redundant but no less damning: "You're not going to give up, are you?!"

The coach, his dad, turns his back and begins to walk toward the bench.

For his mother, the son recollects a roll call at the beginning of a seventh-grade gym class. Distracted, he didn't hear the teacher ask if he were present, so other students' eyes sought him out. When he said, "Here," the cavernous gymnasium ballooned with silence, pierced suddenly by the class clown who screamed, "Guess who's not Lisa's boyfriend anymore!"

Stunned, the boy heard his mind echoing silent shrieks of disbelief, "What? What?" as he fought off the possibility that the only girlfriend he had ever had had dumped him. She had.

He fled from school into a late spring afternoon, a festival of blue and green calling him out. Within, a hand of immobilizing darkness closed on him. A thousand miles home, alone, he wept so that he thought he might be losing his mind.

When his mother arrived from work, she found him in his room, where she initiated a first move in a round of: What's wrong? Nothing. Are you sure?

With repetitions of this loving game, he broke, revealing his consternation and humiliation with another frightening rage of tears.

"I know it feels awful now, but there's more than one fish in the sea," he heard his mother saying. "There are lots of girls out there who are going to like you. You're such a handsome, wonderful boy!"

A bewildered, "What?" eked into his mind. Or was it a shriek? "What? Don't you see what happened to me?"

These many years later, the young man's throat clogs with the sadness of not being known by his mother, who made a heartfelt attempt to rescue him from the incomprehensible moment of a broken heart.

Now, for the first time in years, there is relationship here. The mother and father are experiencing one of life's most dramatic moments. Their son's words are an earthquake, shaking the foundation of how they think about who they are, who he is, and what has been going on all of these years.

In this moment, created in part by their willingness to be touched by their son's plea, they have three choices. First, they can revert to form, behaving naturally as they have in the past, criticizing and reassuring. The risk is recreating the past and rejecting their son.

Second, they can try to stop doing what comes naturally, taking a position at the apologetic extreme ("Oh, we made a mistake. How can we set it right?"). The risk is abandoning themselves.

Third, they can begin with their son to grope toward talking sense — toward the invention of a new behavioral language that allows them to learn together when one or more of them is "lost" or "fractured." Such a journey is at once perilous and thrilling. The natural tendency will be to fight or flee from this unknown internal and interpersonal territory rather than seeking to develop the ability to make new sense of their lives together.

This extraordinary meeting ends with a discussion of these three alternatives, and how the parents might support themselves should they choose the third option. The son makes an appointment to meet with the consultant. The family leaves. Soon after this meeting, the son goes to work in the shipping department of a small company. A few months later, he returns to school, much to the joy and relief of his parents.

Commentary: The Journey

This book describes a journey into a way of thinking that enables us to communicate in a new way, that takes us from an interpersonal world of fault finding and communicating to fix, to a place of joint sense making and communicating to learn. That journey requires personal change, expressed as a set of skills for reflecting on and changing our own thinking and behavior and for enabling others to do the same.

The first two phases of the growth process, discovery and invention, are embedded in the "A Son Drops Out of College" story. These two phases, which involve internal awareness and change, lay the groundwork for interpersonal learning.

Discovery

Behavior follows from thinking and feeling, so if the family members wanted to improve their ongoing communication, they would have to change how they think and feel. But changing in this way without understanding the tacit assumptions that shape their thoughts and feelings would prove exceptionally

Figure I.1 Two Frames of Reference

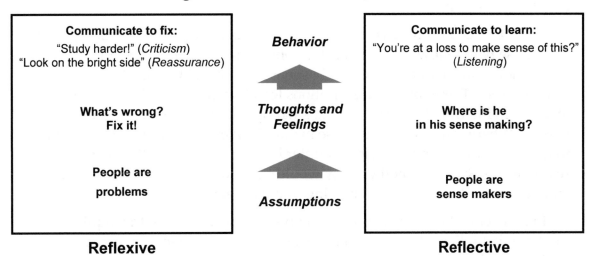

difficult. In the language of this book, they must first become aware of (discover) and then change the very way they make sense of themselves and their relations with one another because we make sense through our thoughts and feelings, along with the assumptions embedded in them.

In effect, the family members would have to discover the causal relationship between behavior, thinking, and feeling, and assumptions depicted in Figure I.1. The left side of the figure presents the "people are problems" assumption that results in their thinking about their son in fault-finding terms ("What's wrong with him, and how do we fix it?"). Because they think of him as a problem, their behavior takes the form of a corrective solution, which itself has two basic forms: criticism or reassurance. These are illustrated by the parents' responses, which precipitate their son's departure: the father is critical ("Study harder") and the mother is reassuring ("Look on the bright side").

In this book, the people-are-problems assumption, the fault finding and deficiency kind of thinking that follows from it, and the resulting corrective behavior (criticism or reassurance) will together be called the *reflexive frame of reference* or *reflexive communication*. This provides a shorthand way of referring to how we think and behave automatically and un-self-consciously, that is, by reflex.

Invention

Along with discovering the frame of reference they are starting from, the family would have to invent and nurture within themselves an alternative frame of reference. The right side of Figure I.1 presents an assumption that people are sense makers, which allows the consultant to think about the son as being stuck in his sense-making process, which enables the father's behavior to be an inquiry

("You're at a loss to make sense of this?") about his son's condition rather than an attempt to fix it.

The father could not have invented this new behavior or the thinking behind it, because both follow from a very different assumption about people than the one he holds: in terms of his son, "My son is a problem" versus "My son is a sense maker." These distinct assumptions lead to contrasting thoughts and feelings. In interrogative form: "What's wrong with my son that I need to fix?" versus "Where is my son in his sense making?" Were the father, mother, and son to transform the drama of their encounter here into change in their everyday relationships with one another, they would have to take on the task of inventing and nurturing their own sense-making frame of reference.

In this book, the assumption that people are sense makers, the inquiry thinking that follows from it, and the consequent interpersonal sense-making skill set will be called a *reflective frame of reference* or *reflective communication*. The word *reflective* designates a way of communicating that is not automatic and must be consciously learned and chosen, through reflection.

In the journey from reflexive to reflective communication, the discovery and invention phases are followed by a second set of phases, practice and action. Essentially, while discovery and invention are about our private, inner worlds, practice and action are about our behavior in the interpersonal world. This book is based on the assumption that we must gain insight into the structure of our inner worlds and reconstruct them in order to make significant changes in our behavior in the interpersonal world. Table I.4 on the next page defines these four phases in greater detail.

Table I.4
Phases of the Journey
from Communicating to Fix to Communicating to Learn

Discovery: Getting Located

We must discover and accept responsibility for the gaps between our ideal and actual communication, to gain insight into the reflexive fault-finding frame of reference that causes them.

Invention: Choosing a Guide

We must invent and learn to trust a reflective sense-making voice that can listen to and question our reflexive interpretations of our internal and interpersonal experience, then assert alternative ways of making sense and behaving.

Practice: Getting Prepared (in a protected setting)

We must practice how to embody in our behavior the values of open agendas, disclosure, and listening and then evaluate and adjust our new behavior with the guidance of a reflective voice (our own or a partner's).

Action: Walking the Talk (in the real world)

We must act to move our communication from a fault-finding (reflexive) frame of reference to a sense making (reflective) one, and renew this intention through a continuous cycle of discovery, invention, practice, and action.

Should you embark on the journey from reflexive to reflective communication, you will venture in intra/interpersonal territory that other authors have named with different concepts. Table I.5 on the next page acknowledges other theorists who describe and explain two fundamentally different ways of making sense and acting in the world.

Table I.5 Theories of Making Sense	
Author and Book	**Two Different Ways of Making Sense and Acting in the World**
Talk Sense, by organizational consultant Barry Jentz	Reflexive versus reflective
Getting to Yes, by negotiators Roger Fisher and William Ury	Hard style—soft style versus win-win style
Megatrends, by futurist John Naisbitt	Either-or versus multiple options
Power and Influence, by business school professor John Kotter	Innocence-cynicism versus beyond naiveté and cynicism
Reflective Practitioner, by philosopher and educator Donald Schön	Technical rationality versus reflection in action
Mindfulness, by social psychologist Ellen Langer	Mindless versus mindful, and automatic versus conscious
Seven Habits of Highly Successful People, by consultant Steven Covey	Dependent-independent versus interdependent

Chapter One

Discovery: Getting Located

Unknowingly, we participate in a set of discrepancies on three levels: assumptions, sense making, and behavior. We are generally quite unaware of dramatic gaps between the assumption about others we believe we make versus actually make, how we believe we make sense versus how we actually make sense, and how we believe we behave versus how we actually behave. "The Lost Hiker Story" illustrates the act of discovery and what it has to do with getting located.

Story: The Lost Hiker

An inexperienced hiker is lost in the woods and does not know yet that he is actually lost. We know he is lost because we are above him in a helicopter and see he is walking in circles. There is a discrepancy between where the hiker actually is and where he thinks he is.

The hiker must do one thing before he can find his way out of the forest other than by chance. It is not to use a compass or try to get help. The hiker cannot take these sensible actions until he makes new sense of where he is. The new sense he must make is, "I am lost."

It is not enough simply to realize that he is lost because the word *realize* does not capture fully the significance of what he must do. He must make a commitment and declare, "I am lost." Ambivalence ("Maybe I'm lost, maybe I'm not") will not do because then he would be in emotional limbo. No effective action follows from emotional limbo, and he needs to take effective action.

He must make a frightening discovery: "I am lost!"

First Discrepancy: What We Assume About Others versus Think We Assume

When the "A Son Drops Out of College" story ends, the parents are lost. For a moment at least, they have discovered that they are not where they thought they were in relationship to their son. In the language of this book, they assumed that they had been relating to him reflectively (people are sense makers), taking him into account as a separate person with a legitimately different way of making sense, when in fact they were relating to him reflexively (people are problems), treating him as a fault to be fixed.

We too must make the discovery that we relate to people through the assumption that people are problems, not through the assumption that people are sense makers. Unless we know where we are starting from, we cannot get where we want to go.

In the following story, see if you do not discover yourself responding to June, the prospective rental client, from this simplistic, reflexive assumption about social reality: "You should see what I see and make the same sense. If you don't, then, what's wrong with you, that I need to fix?"

Story: The Cord of Wood

As the new owner of a rental home on Nantucket Island, Terry received a telephone call from June, who was interested in renting the last two weeks of September, a difficult time to book, so he was excited about the potential booking and the possibility of developing a September clientele for a property that rented mainly during July and August. He described his year-round home, picturing the physical setting, the layout of rooms, contents, electric heating, and so on. He told June that he would not provide wood for the wood stove in the living room, wanting to save himself the trouble of locating firewood and getting it to the house (he lived off island and did not yet know anyone on island who could help supply the wood). This was not a problem for the renter, who agreed to book the two weeks. The next day, Terry reconsidered the firewood decision and spent the better part of a day arranging for wood to be delivered to the house, at a cost of $350 for a half-cord! He called June to tell her of her good fortune. The two had talked by phone only two days before and agreed to dates and price, but Terry did not have a signed lease as of his second call.

"Hello, June. This is Terry McDean. I'm delighted to tell you that contrary to what I told you two days ago, there will be firewood at the house for the wood stove. And I want you to feel free to use as much of it as you like."

"Oh. Okay," June said, hesitatingly, her voice trailing off.

Terry thought, "What's her problem?" He was caught off guard by her apparent uncertainty. He decided to reveal his surprise and inquire about what he heard in her tone.

"I'm a little surprised. You seem uncertain."

"No. No." She paused. Then she said haltingly, "That's good."

"That's a mixed message!" Terry thought. In her quiet way she sounded resoundingly ambivalent. He was uncertain about how to make sense of it and what to do. He decided to give her information about his uncertainty and its origin.

"It's me who's uncertain now. I guess I expected that you'd be pleased, and you don't seem to be."

"But I have two young children," June said, with certainty trailing off to a tacit interrogative.

What does having children have to do with firewood? Terry was annoyed but more confused than annoyed. He committed himself not to run from his confusion into anger, blaming her for elliptical speech.

He said, "Yes, I remember you said you have two young children."

"I don't want them to get sick!" was June's reply.

Now Terry wondered, "Firewood? Children? Get sick? What are you talking about? I provide wood and you're telling me you don't want your kids to get cold and sick? Give me a break!" Again, he decided to pass on his accusatory thoughts, reminding himself that he might not be able to make sense of June's utterances other than in negative terms, but surely if he could see matters from her perspective, there would be sense there. He continued, "I don't want them to get sick either. Still, you're concerned that they might, having to do with something I don't understand. Can you help me understand your concern?"

June was quick to respond: "They're just babies, you know, and I go out of my way to keep them warm. You did say that it could be cold there in late September, didn't you?"

"Oh, that's it!" Terry thought. "The woman is nuts! I'm giving her an additional way to heat the house, and she's talking about her kids getting sick from the cold. What's missing here?" Stepping back from his inner harangue, he forced himself to reflect: "Stop trying to figure out what she is not talking about! Focus on what she has said and inquire. Apparently she is frightened about her kids getting cold and sick, and in some way she is relating these possibilities to the wood. Inquire about these apparent connections."

"I did say it could be cold," Terry responded. "But it could be quite warm too. June, I may be searching here, but it seems that in some way the wood has raised a question in your mind and a fear about keeping your kids warm?"

Emphatically, June proclaimed, "Yes, it has! It has indeed!" She stopped, as if that were enough to clear up the matter. It was difficult for Terry not to retreat into the right-wrong frame of reference that either he must be stupid or she must be stupid, or deceptive, or purposefully difficult.

Again, Terry gathered himself to assert his confusion instead of blaming her: "I'm blind to the connection, because I keep thinking that I'm giving you an additional way to heat the house."

There was a long silence before she began cautiously, even incredulously, to edge out through her own fear of looking stupid: "You mean . . . But aren't you asking me not to . . . Oh, I thought you were asking me not to turn on the central heating. But are you?"

Terry blurted, "No! That never crossed my mind!"

"I'm afraid I jumped to a conclusion," June said apologetically.

"June, it never crossed my mind. I called assuming the wood would make the house charming, more pleasurable for you — make you enjoy your stay and want to come back again!"

Again, there was a long pause before she decided to reveal her thoughts: "You're not going to believe this, but when you said you had the wood, I decided right then not to come. I've been sitting here planning to return the lease unsigned!"

"Terrific! I wouldn't have known if you hadn't told me."

June paused, then said slowly, "That's the very last thing I would ever have told you."

"Somehow, I got a sense of that," Terry said, unsuccessfully trying for a light touch in tone.

Silence again.

June poked cautiously into the silence: "You're going to think I'm crazy for asking this. You're not asking me to keep the heating off, are you?"

"No, June, I'm not."

"Okay. I needed to be reassured," she said.

"I've got a question for you. Was there anything in our prior conversation that led you to think I was asking you not to use the central heating?"

With certainty, June asserted, "No. When you called today about the wood, it seemed so obvious that you must have gotten nervous about the cost of the electricity. I know Nantucket. I know the electricity costs!"

Still incredulous, Terry asked, "Does it make sense that what was on my mind was how to make this house so appealing that you will want to come back again?"

"It does now, but not when the conversation began."

Commentary

It is very difficult to read this story and not feel the pull of our reflexive assumption that people are problems, writing June off as up to no good of some kind, or obtuse, or a loony. In effect, our reflexive voice, like the reflexive voice in Terry, expects June to see what we saw and make the same sense of it that we did (a cord of wood should bring pleasure and a return rental). When she does not, we tend to wonder what's wrong with her and how to get her straightened out. That is, the very nature of our reflexive thinking is to assume that people should make sense the way we do, not differently. A difference in sense making is something that should not exist and ought to be corrected rather than something that is legitimate and needs to be understood.

Terry's reflexive thought and accompanying irritation, confusion, and anger are evident in these two examples of his internal monologue:

- "Firewood? Children? Get sick? What are you talking about? I provide wood, and you're telling me you don't want your kids to get cold and sick? Give me a break!"

- "The woman is nuts! I'm giving her an additional way to heat the house, and she's talking about her kids getting sick from the cold. What's missing here?"

Again and again, Terry turns away from his reflexive urge to write off June because she is not making the same sense he is making. In effect, he turns away from his reflexive voice's assumption that social reality is a simple matter of two people looking at the same thing and making the same sense. This view of social reality is pictured in the "Reflexive Event Cartoon" shown here. The initiator of the interaction assumes that the receiver is looking at the same event and making the same sense as the initiator.

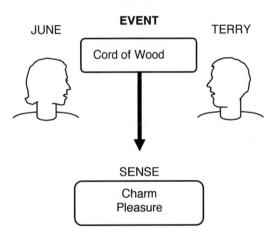

Reflexive Event Cartoon

When Terry turns away from his reflexive urge, he turns toward reflective inquiry and demonstrates in his responses to June how we might learn about rather than write off another person's different sense making. Here are three examples:

- He decided to pass on his accusatory thoughts, reminding himself that he might not be able to make sense of June's utterances other than in negative terms, but surely if he could see matters from her perspective, there would be sense there.

- Stepping back from his inner harangue, he forced himself to reflect: "Stop trying to figure out what she is not talking about! Focus on what she has said and inquire. Apparently she is frightened about her kids getting cold and sick, and in some way she is relating these possibilities to the wood. Inquire about these apparent connections."

- It was difficult for Terry not to retreat into the right-wrong frame of reference that either he must be stupid or she must be stupid, or deceptive, or purposefully difficult.

In effect, he acts on the reflective assumption that people are sense makers, from which follows the complex view of social reality pictured in the "Reflective Event Cartoon." In this cartoon there is not one "sense" box but two, depicting two people looking at the same event and making sense differently. Terry acts on the reflective imperative not to correct June, but to understand June's different way of making sense before he decides how to respond. (To seek to understand by listening is not to agree. The other person's different sense making can be legitimate yet limited in its nature and incorrect in its outcome.) In this way, he earns her trust, gains understanding, and saves a business deal that was falling apart.

Reflective Event Cartoon

EVENT

JUNE   TERRY

The Cord of Wood

SENSE   SENSE

Don't turn on the central heating
It will be cold
Kids will get sick
Return the lease unsigned
He's out to cheat me

Charm
Pleasure
Return contract
I'm doing her a favor

Yes, But: Skepticism About Time

The "Cord of Wood" story is low-hanging fruit for the skeptic in us, particularly regarding the issue of time. Skepticism about the relationship between reflective skills and time ("wasting it," "taking too much of it," and "not having it to invest in such a slow process") is the most persistent objection to reflective skills. (Additional skeptical concerns are addressed in Chapter Five.) There are two predictable skeptical responses to the story here.

The first objection is that Terry should have begun by telling June that the wood was for pleasure, not for heat. Then he wouldn't have wasted his time or hers. This objection makes good sense, but could be voiced only after reading the whole story through to the punch line. Terry would have had to be omniscient to know ahead of time that June might make sense of his offer of the cord of wood as a request not to use the central heating. In fact, if he were to have made such an unlikely anticipation, it would not have been normal practice. Normal (time-saving) practice, called reflexive practice here, follows from the assumption that two people looking at the same event will see the event similarly: because Terry meant the cord of wood to be pleasure, that's how June would perceive it. By contrast, predicting that two people looking at the same event will see it differently is reflective thinking. So this objection to the slow pace of interaction in the story isn't a normal practice time saver at all.

The second objection could be stated in this way: "Granted we all start off badly on occasion. He should have said, 'June, what's the problem?' Then they straighten out the misunderstanding and get off the phone." Early in the conversation, Terry might have said to June, "What's the problem?" In response, June might have said, "The wood stove won't heat the house. I need to use the central heating." Quickly they could have jointly seen and avoided the lengthy misunderstanding in the story. However, it is more likely that June would have said, "There's no problem," for from the moment Terry first spoke, she had decided to send the lease back after the call ended, and she is clearly loath to reveal that decision. Were she to say back to Terry, "There's no problem" or something like it, Terry would face the same difficult situation he encounters in the story as written.

As illustrated in these two attempts to save time, our attempts are often at odds with the actual outcome.

Second Discrepancy: How We Make Sense versus Think We Make Sense

There is a critical moment in all of our lives when we can gain awareness of how reflexive (closed) our sense making can be, even as we like to think about our sense making and behavior as reflective (open). That moment is when someone catches us off guard with negative information about our performance. We are stung, when only a second before we were at ease. In our alerted condition, it is not the reflective (open) part of us who fills our minds with exploratory thoughts about the nature of the information giver's sense making. It is the defensive, reflexive voice in us that takes command.

In the "Your Spanish Is Getting Worse!" story that follows, the lead character is caught off guard by negative information about her performance and reacts reflexively, as we all would.[1] We see her in the act of discovery, that is, of finding herself entrapped in her reflexive sense making. She extricates herself and demonstrates reflective sense making.

Story: Your Spanish Is Getting Worse!

I am a Mexican who, at the age of forty, decided to go to graduate school and do my dissertation on the topic of turnover in Mexican workers employed by American firms in Mexico. It is a topic of great interest to the managers in these firms because turnover is very high and costly. After three years of preliminary research, lining up eight firms to participate in my study, and spending a year in Mexico collecting data, I returned to the United States to develop a method for analyzing the data.

Then I discovered I had a serious cancer, calling for hospitalization, chemotherapy, and radiation treatments. The doctors thought I was going to die. I thought I was going to die. Fighting the disease took all of my energy and attention for a full year, and even then, when the disease disappeared with the same stealth that it arrived, I was on a five-years-until-you-know-you'll-live remission schedule. Still, having spent a year with death, I chose life.

After that year's absence, I returned to Mexico to make a presentation about my research at a national convention and to meet with all of the plant managers together to explain why I had been so long in returning and express my regret about keeping them waiting so long for results, update them on the statistical methodology I'd developed to analyze their data, and ask for their help in giving me additional data to complete the study. This meeting seemed to go well. The managers were sympathetic to my plight and enthusiastic about the methodology and the results it promised to produce. Of course, they were disappointed that I had been so long in returning to them.

By prior agreement, my presentation to the group of plant managers was followed by a one-on-one meeting with each of them. The first of these meetings was with a Mexican manager of a plant employing fifteen thousand people (the largest plant in my study). This woman and plant were very important to me because my methodology depended on having a very large plant, a very small plant, and others of varying sizes between the extremes.

Little did I know that I was in for a shocking surprise. The plant manager began by saying, "Nice to see you. Welcome to Chihuahua." Then, leaning toward me, she spoke with voluble aggressiveness: "I have to be honest with you. The meeting you had with all of the participants in the study was a waste of time. A year has gone by, and I'm amazed that you have no news for us. And besides, your Spanish is getting worse!"

A chasm of stunned silence yawned between us.

"Well? Well!?" Her voice, a fist, smashed me into stupefied silence.

My first thought was of croaking myself because I'd failed. My urge was to apologize: how could I expect these people to understand what I'd been through? My second sensation was to choke her. I was angry and wanted to strike back.

The researcher describes reflexive sense making graphically through two contrasting metaphors of croaking *on self-doubt or* choking *the plant manager with an accusatory outburst. Automatically, her sense making is either-or in nature: either doubt the self or blame the other. Although the two voices speak different words and point toward action in opposite directions, they are inextricably linked as one voice, two sides of the same coin, so to speak, not different coins. Reflexive sense making and behavior is either-or in nature: fight-flight, right-wrong, accept-reject, and so on.*

I was drowning in a molasses of doubt and outrage when my mind seized on the idea that when I am caught off guard and hurt by what someone says, I automatically attribute conscious negative intent (darkness) to the person who spoke, when, even as I experience the behavior as darkness, the other person might see the behavior arising out of positive intent (lightness), or the person might be in the grip of forces beyond the person's control.

Here, we see the researcher thinking from a reflective frame of reference: Where am I in my sense making? She turns inward, identifying a pattern in her mental behavior of attributing conscious negative intent when she is hurt by feedback from the plant manager. By identifying her reflexive pattern of thinking, then questioning it by raising possible alternative causes for the plant manager's behavior, she is making a choice to separate herself from her reflexive thinking.

Her seizing on the idea of possible alternative causation is emotionally akin to dragging herself from the primordial ooze of her reflexive sense making. That ooze is "a molasses of doubt and outrage" that expresses itself as flight behavior (croak apologize) or fight behavior (choke attack). Under the conditions, this moment of stepping back from her initial, reflexive sense making is remarkable.

Reflective sense making is not a reflex. It is a choice. It insists on questioning the correctness of our automatic (reflexive) sense making. Initial either-or sense (croak-choke) is put on hold rather than accepted as given truth. Then attention is turned away from self, toward the other person: Where is the plant manager in her sense making?

In the silence of my own mind, I forced myself to ask, "Where is she [the plant manager] in her sense making? What sense is coming through in the tone? She is disappointed in me in getting no results."

The researcher demonstrates her reflective knowledge that people are sense makers. We make sense of the world through our thoughts and feelings, expectations, intents, needs, hopes, fears, yearnings, and the assumptions embedded in them. To understand a person's attempt to communicate with us, we must not take his or her words literally but inquire about the sense the person may be trying to communicate. Our inquiry takes place first in our own minds, then through testing our sense of what's being communicated.

Next, the researcher takes her internal reflective inquiry into the interpersonal world, testing her inferences with the plant manager so the researcher can confirm whether she understands the sense that the plant manager intended to convey.

When I finally spoke into the silence, I struggled to say to her, "Thank you for your directness. You are disappointed because you expected I would have something different to offer and not take so much time?"

The plant manager's tone shifted from aggressiveness to neediness as she said, "You bet I did. We are in a mess. We need help now! Turnover is increasing, and we don't know what to do. And you talk about a 'methodology to analyze data.'"

I was tempted to speak from my reflexes — "Oh, I'm sorry you're still mad at me (croaking)" or "Don't blame me for your problems (choking)!" Instead, I asked myself, What sense does she make of being in this mess? Then the obvious hit me: She's in a predicament and wishing for a fix.

So I asked, "You were looking for answers and didn't get them?"

"Yes, I was. I haven't the slightest idea why the other managers were excited by the methodology. I need help!" she said.

By this point in the conversation, I wasn't paying so much attention to my automatic mind, though it was still talking ("Maybe I didn't present it clearly enough [self-doubt]?" or "What's your problem? The other managers understood it [blame]!" Instead, I was imagining what she was saying about where she was in her sense making. She seemed lost, unable to figure out why the other managers responded excitedly to my presentation.

So I inquired, "The conversation about the methodology didn't make any sense and so wasn't useful?"

"That's right! Exactly! What was all the excitement about?"

"I would enjoy telling you!" I said with enthusiasm.

I tend to launch enthusiastically into explanations, but I stopped, and, throttling my desire to expound, I alerted myself to set up a structure of next steps that we both understood. Because of the limit on our time that day, I suggested that we begin our work in the twenty minutes remaining, then make an hour appointment for the next day when I would help her understand the methodology. If she needed more time, I told her I would arrange for a colleague of mine in Mexico to help her further because I had to return home in two days.

As I began to walk the plant manager through the content from the prior meeting, explaining how the methodology would yield the answers she was looking for, I learned two crucial things. She was the only plant manager in the group who did not have a background in statistics, so could not understand the content or significance of my progress report. Had she not revealed her vulnerability to me, I could not have gotten her help in understanding statistics, and she would have lost the opportunity to get the results of the study. And, incredibly, she had decided to drop out of the study and inform me of her decision by fax after I returned to the United States. I would have lost three years of work toward my Ph.D. because the methodology was invalid without a large manufacturing site.

Commentary

We tend to think of our sense making as open, subject to examination and change, and we think of the person who tells us what we do not want to hear as closed or defensive (reflexive). The researcher illustrates this generalization vividly at the beginning of the interaction where the plant manager first speaks. The researcher understandably feels victimized. She is there to be open and helpful, and clearly the plant manager attacks her.

Remarkably, the researcher does not respond to the perceived attack with a return attack (or apology), justifying it by attributing conscious negative intent to the plant manager. That would have been normal behavior under these conditions. Instead, she turns her attention away from the plant manager's action and toward questioning her own sense making. She discovers that she is making sense by using only either-or categories. Her unclouded discovery of her real starting place, a closed, defensive, reflexive frame of reference, is what positions her to choose to reframe the situation from reflexive (closed) to reflective (open).

Under the pressure of receiving negative information about our performance, all of us reflexively attribute conscious negative intent to the other person and declare our innocence. The researcher shows us the error in this thinking and how to correct it: we must take responsibility for our own reflexive sense making (closed) before we can be where we think we are already: open or reflective.

Third Discrepancy: How We Behave versus Think We Behave

We like to think that our behavior reflects open agendas, giving good feedback, and listening. But when we are under pressure, we tend to do the opposite: act from closed agendas, withhold information, and criticize or reassure rather than listen. If we can recognize the discrepancy between how we think we behave and actually behave, we open a window of discovery into its causation: our reflexive fix-it frame of reference.

The following story "Are You Calling Me a Liar?" is meant to show how we naturally (reflexively) handle a difficult interpersonal situation. The lead character faces the most common of all difficult interpersonal situations: all of us have had to disclose information to someone about their behavior or performance that we have withheld for months, even years. This happens in relation to our intimates at home, employees, and colleagues at work.

At first, we might be annoyed by someone's behavior or attitude. The incident is but a disappearing sound in the orchestration of a busy day. With repetition, though, the scratching sound of the behavior or attitude becomes the constant scrape of a negative pattern. We hope it will go away. Yes, we should talk to the person, now, not put it off, and yet we do put off giving the bad news. Other priorities call. We hate to confront difficult performance issues. They're very messy.

When the scraping sound turns into an intolerable screech, it forces us to act. We are then in a predicament of practical and ethical difficulty: we have withheld a lot of information, probably while espousing the value of trust through openness. Now we must ask the other person to listen and, often, to change.

Story: Are You Calling Me a Liar? (Reflexive Version)

Mitch Andrews is a talented and accomplished graphic artist who was once employed in the defense industry.[2] He moved from southern California to Arizona, where he took the job of graphic artist for Pecos Inc., a large mail order company. Mitch reported to the vice president for client services, who also supervised the print department.

Mitch's illustration, design, and layout work pleased the vice president, although she and other vice presidents and managers occasionally were disappointed by what appeared to be poor coordination between Mitch and the print shop, evident through printing defects and delays. Mitch himself suggested a solution: why not merge graphic arts and the print shop into one publications department, and promote Mitch to manager? After a time, the vice president agreed. Soon after, she left the company when the CEO retired.

A year passed with an acting CEO and a new boss for Mitch before a permanent CEO took office, bringing with him a new vice president of client services, to whom he assigned the publications department, still with Mitch as manager.

Bill Travis was on the job scarcely a week before complaints about the publications department began to reach him. He contacted Mitch's former bosses and heard evidence of two major problems: Mitch appeared to play favorites in print job scheduling and pricing, and when speaking with customers, he blamed the printers for production problems that resulted from his own decision making.

Bill decided to try to start on a positive note with Mitch. He called a meeting to voice general expectations for the publications department. Without sharing specific complaints, Bill simply suggested that it was important that publications provide consistent, uniform services, with no favoritism in scheduling or pricing. He also emphasized how important it was that customers be able to trust fully whatever they might hear from the publications department. Mitch agreed and left Bill's office.

Nevertheless, over the next several months the complaints continued. Finally, even print shop staff and Mitch's secretary came to Bill to report inappropriate behavior. Furthermore, they reported that Mitch would grow livid when they tried to suggest operational improvements. Bill shared his growing concern with the CEO, who suggested that a talented artist might not have the temperament to be a good manager. At last, Bill decided he had to call a meeting with Mitch to discuss the problem more openly and directly.

"Come in, Mitch. Have a seat."

"Thanks. What's up?"

"You know, we had a talk a few months ago about my expectations for the publications department . . ."

Mitch interrupted, saying positively, "You bet, and it helped a lot."

"I'm not so sure about that. I've been getting disturbing calls lately."

"About the department? Well, we have little problems, but nothing I can't handle," Mitch said confidently.

Bill decided to stop beating around the bush: "Mitch, are you dishonest?"

Appearing flabbergasted, Mitch barked, "What? Who says that?"

"Never mind that. Let's just say that I'm hearing it from a number of sources," Bill said, not giving him an easy way out.

"I resent that! I resent your not telling me who says these things!"

"The important thing is whether it's true. Do you lie to customers?" Bill said, holding Mitch's feet to the fire.

"What? Are *you* calling me a liar?" Mitch almost shouted, continuing to feign indignation.

"No, Mitch, I'm just trying to get at the facts."

"I'll tell you the facts! Ever since I took over the publications department two years ago, it's been one manager after another out to get me! You come into this company not knowing a thing about the problems I face, and you start listening to all these complaints from people who don't know anything about the printing business! It isn't fair!"

Bill heard him making excuses and said, "It's not fair that the department doesn't deliver what you promise on time!"

"Who says that? I always deliver what I promise!" Mitch exclaimed.

"And the word I get . . . do you play favorites in pricing?" Bill figured Mitch needed to hear the whole thing, and when he did, he hammered back: "How would anyone know that? What does anyone around here know about print job pricing? What do *you* know about printing? What are *your* qualifications to sit in judgment? Have you ever run a printing operation?"

"What I know," returned Bill, "is that you're nearly hysterical right now and that you're yelling at your boss. I don't much like that! In fact, I'm beginning to agree with the CEO that you may not belong in a management position!"

"The CEO! Well, I can see how the deck is stacked, and I don't much like *that!* I'm not going to put up with it! As far as I'm concerned, this meeting is over! If you want to see me again, I'll be bringing my attorney!"

In fact, Mitch ultimately does bring his attorney to a meeting with Bill.

Commentary: The Skill Gap

We like to think that our behavior reflects a commitment to learning with others and that our communication is skillful and effective. We believe that we allow joint participation in setting agendas, let others know the data from which we are reasoning, and listen to others' perspectives. But we do not. And this major discrepancy in our behavior represents a skill gap that has a devastating effect on our ability to achieve the results we want with others.

Why such a gap between our intentions and our skills? When we feel we have much at stake, our patterns of natural, reflexive behavior are triggered, and we find ourselves communicating in an unskilled manner, characterized by:

- Closed agendas. We structure to keep agendas closed by not revealing our purposes and procedures (methods, tactics).

- Withholding information: We withhold observable data while revealing only our opinions or conclusions, and we tend to keep our sense making private rather than asserting it for inquiry.

- Criticizing or reassuring: We criticize or reassure people when they present their side of things rather than listen.

These reflexive behaviors are illustrated in Bill's first two meetings with Mitch. At the first meeting, he decided to start on a positive note with Mitch. He called a meeting to voice general expectations for the publications department. Without sharing specific complaints, Bill simply suggested that it was important that the department provide consistent, uniform services, with no favoritism in scheduling or pricing. He also emphasized how important it was that customers be able to trust fully whatever they might hear from the department.

In other words, to start on a positive note, he did not set out the real agenda of the meeting or disclose any of the observable data reported to him about Mitch's performance. In effect, Bill simply stated general goals—for example, "consistent, uniform service, with no favoritism in scheduling and pricing"—that Mitch embraced without knowing what Bill was really getting at.

When starting on a positive note failed to change Mitch's behavior, Bill switched to the get-tough approach, deciding to discuss the problem more openly and directly. To do so, he disclosed only inferences about Mitch's performance without the observational data reported to him (as a result, Mitch could hear the inferences only as accusations). He did not listen to Mitch, nor had he structured the agenda so Mitch might know what was going on and why. He simply launched into a pattern of indirect questioning, an effort that yielded an attorney in attendance at his next meeting with Mitch.

We'll revisit this story later to illustrate another way Bill could handle the interaction, making use of the three crucial interpersonal sense-making skills:

- Structuring for open agendas

- Giving good information

- Listening, or getting good information

Each of these skills will be defined and explored in depth in Chapters Three and Four. However, these are not skills in the typical sense. Reflexively, the word *skill* connotes a picture of a tool that can be picked up and put down, disconnected from the process that produced it. It is assumed that a skill can be added to a current repertoire with minimal self-examination, insight, and change in the person who will use the skill.

In contrast, from a reflective perspective, a skill is not a static tool. Like the branches of a tree, it cannot be disconnected from its larger part that is underground and out of sight, or from the process of growth. The larger part of a reflective skill is the personal thinking and feeling from which the skill follows and the person's assumptions, which gives rise to the thinking and feeling.

Why Is Discovering Where We Are So Hard—and So Important?

The prior stories show that we participate in a set of discrepancies between how we think we communicate and how we actually do.

The continuing story of "The Lost Hiker" again serves to illustrate why the act of discovery, that is, encountering and accepting our participation in discrepancies, is so difficult. Discovery requires facing our fear that we may not be what we believe ourselves to be. The anticipation of this fear repels us, so we close off awareness of discrepancies rather than open to them.

Story: The Lost Hiker, *Continued*

Let us return to our helicopter, and once again observe from above the lost hiker who does not recognize that he is lost. The hiker needs to take effective action in order to find his way out of the woods. But he won't be able to until he discovers the sense of "I am lost." Observing him, we can agree on the one thing the hiker needs to do but least wants to do: he does not want to say to himself, "I am lost" because he has a great deal invested in holding onto the sense that he is not lost and too much to lose by admitting that he is lost.

The experience of being lost does not exist as an isolated piece of information inside him. It is linked to other emotions and thoughts:

- To be lost could be tantamount to being stupid. This could take the form of shouting at himself, "If you're so smart, what are you doing going around in circles? You stupid fool. What did you think you were doing coming out here!" He might be filled with self-disgust or shame.

- To be lost could equal being incompetent. "If you're so competent, why'd you screw up? You always think you know what you're doing, but you don't! Why weren't you better prepared?" He might be filled with self-hate or humiliation.

- To be lost could be experienced as giving up and thereby being irresponsible to the sacred dictate: "Never quit!" If so, he might be vulnerable to a threat of cowardice. Only cowards give up. This threat could excite his worst fear: that he is once and for all a sniveling weakling. He might be filled with terror or be engulfed by a sense of loss.

So the potential cost of declaring, "I am lost," feels very high. But if he cannot ease into an emerging sense of "I am lost," paradoxically experiencing his acknowledgment as a strength, and if he instead continues to hold sacred the sense that he is not lost, he will go around in circles indefinitely.

Commentary

The moral of the lost hiker is simple and provocative: what the hiker most needs to do, he least wants to do. In effect, what the hiker most needs to do in the interest of his own learning and consequent survival is to say to himself, "I am lost." But he least wants to do that because he is entrapped by emotionally held assumptions that it would be an admission of stupidity, or incompetence, or cowardice, or weakness. Powerful forces act to blind him to the discrepancy in which he exists, that he is going around in circles, lost; but in his own mind, he is not lost.

Paradoxically, he must declare that he is lost before he can begin to locate himself and find his way.

"The Lost Hiker" story shows why it is so hard to discover ourselves where we really are but do not want to be — in a set of discrepancies between our idealized and actual selves:

- We believe that we have an assumption that other people have a different perspective than we do, and we advocate taking those perspectives into account, even as we actually operate on an assumption that others see the world as we do (or should).

- We believe we are open and reflective in our sense making, even as we react reflexively and cling to a fix-it mode of thinking.

- We believe our behavior skillfully reflects using open agendas, disclosing information, and listening, even as we actually use closed agendas, withhold information, and criticize or reassure people, a major discrepancy we will call the *skill gap*.

Discovering where we are, as hard as it is, leads us to want to close that gap and change the way we behave in communication with others. But there is no shortcut to new interpersonal behavior.

Before we can embody authentic reflective skills, we must gain self-knowledge about our habitual patterns of behavior and their underlying causation in a reflexive frame of reference. With that understanding, we can then choose to invent a reflective inner voice to guide us as we learn and apply the new skills of talking sense. That is the work of the next phase: invention.

Chapter Two

Invention: Choosing a Guide

When life brings us face to face with discrepancies between our idealized and actual selves, we will think reflexively, "What's wrong with me that I am here?" We will either flee from the discrepancies or fight off the information or person who triggered the pain we feel. To stop the flight or fight and surrender to the confusion and the searching for sense that accompanies discovery could be experienced as proof that we are less than we had thought ourselves to be.

In order to move forward and benefit from discovering our reflexive frame of reference, we must invent and nurture a new reflective voice. As only one example, when we hear our reflexive voice saying, "What's wrong with me that I am here?" we must have at the ready a confident, reflective voice that can say, "Nothing may be wrong at all. I may simply be frightened by what I see."

The invention and nurturing of a new relationship to the reflexive part of our minds seems to require an interpersonal experience: we need to take part in an interaction with someone who can relate to our reflexive selves from a reflective frame of reference. That is what happens in the next two stories. In both, the main characters' internal conversations are dominated by their reflexive voices. Through interaction with the consultant from "A Son Drops Out of College," who relates to them from a reflective frame of reference, they begin to invent their own reflective voices that in time can relate as equals with their reflexive voices.

In each story, it will be apparent that the process of reflective learning that is portrayed here as two distinct phases, discovery and invention, is more of a continuum. Although invention follows discovery, it also enables it. This relationship is clarified by the general idea that to know a place we are in, we must leave it for someplace different and then return to know the original place in a new way.

Our starting place is our reflexive frame. To discover it, we must leave it, step outside of it. Doing so requires the existence of a different reflective place to step onto. But that different place does not exist in our minds because we have not invented it yet. It is provided initially by the reflective voice and behavior of a person with whom we interact. As a result of the interaction, we begin to internalize that external voice and make it our own.

Story: So I'm Not Stupid?

The lead character here, Ben, is the son from the "A Son Drops Out of College" story. He talks with the consultant from that story, who helps him discover and take responsibility for his crippling attitude toward himself as a person who cannot make sense. The two began to talk the week after the meeting between Ben and his parents.

After getting reacquainted and talking about the four-way meeting, Ben turns the conversation back to his test problem: "I don't know what to think. My roommate studies half as hard as I do and doesn't know the stuff. I sit next to him during a test, listening to his pencil scratching back and forth on the paper. The longer I sit, the louder it gets. Can you believe, he passes!"

As Ben stops talking, he slouches into the armchair, throwing one leg up over an arm. He looks at the consultant, anticipating a response. The consultant, imagining what appears to be the effect of these classroom events on Ben, asks, "It's more than frustrating. You begin to doubt yourself."

"You bet I do. I know the stuff. I study with four other guys on my floor, and they all ask me for help! But on the tests, I can't deliver!"

It appears to the consultant that Ben cannot understand his classroom experience. Rather than assume that this inference is correct and then privately decide how to get Ben out of such an undesirable place, the consultant tests his inference: "So, you can't make heads or tails of this?"

"No, I can't. I'm as smart as they are! What's my problem?"

Ben appears to be at once stuck and furious for being so. Instead of reflexively trying to get him out of that place, the consultant tries to acknowledge Ben where he is: "You seem stuck and furious with yourself for it?"

"That's right! Exactly! W hat's wrong with me!" Ben appears to confirm being stuck and angry. He wants no part of being stuck. It's too painful to be there because the meaning to him of being stuck seems to be failure.

"You've got yourself sized up as a failure?" The consultant tries to recognize and legitimize Ben for where he appears to be in his own assessment of himself: a failure. Paradoxically, until he is accepted for where he is and as a result arrives there himself, he cannot leave that place. He will experience any attempt to take him out of what he is in as a violation of his integrity and will resist it.

Responding to the consultant's question, "You've got yourself sized up as a failure?" Ben asks, "Wouldn't you?"

"No," says the consultant. "You seem ashamed because you can't sort yourself out here. There's no shame in being stuck. Getting stuck happens—that is, if you risk any kind of movement." Here, the consultant shifts from listening to Ben's experience, as evidenced in his prior responses:

- "It's more than frustrating. You begin to doubt yourself?"

- "So you can't make heads or tails of this?"

- "You seem stuck."

He now presents the reflective relationship to "no sense" (I can be stuck and not be ashamed) in contrast to Ben's reflexive relationship (I am stuck so I must be ashamed).

But Ben is not ready to entertain an alternative relationship to himself as a person who is stuck. He still wants to flee the place. He pleads, "Yeah, but how do I get out of this mess?"

"Wish there were an easy way out?" the consultant asks, smiling.

Ben bursts out, "Sure!"

"When wishing doesn't work, you slap yourself around, right?"

Exasperated, Ben says, "Yes! I can't figure it out! I should have!"

"And you think there is something wrong with you because you can't get it done alone?"

"Yes. Yes, I do."

For the first extended period of time, Ben sits silently, apparently reflecting on the commitment he has just made.

By saying "Yes. Yes, I do," he is putting his feet down, making a commitment. Commitment is the act of immersing the whole self in a position. Here, that position is, "Because I can't figure it out alone, there is something wrong with me." Paradoxically, immersion does not produce drowning and blindness to other perspectives, as we would logically predict. It can produce distance (that is, perspective) and insight.

When Ben says, "Yes. Yes, I do" and then pauses, he comes through the fear of making a commitment to find new questions for himself on the other side. He can ask himself: Do I really believe there is something wrong with me because I couldn't figure it out alone? Asking this question is an act of separating himself from the position or assumption itself. It becomes a subject of inquiry where before it was an object embedded in his person, controlling him and yet beyond his control. In effect, his question raises the possibility of insight into the assumption that began to exist as his only in the instant he said "Yes. Yes, I do."

After several seconds of silence, Ben continues, revealing the pain bedeviling his existence: "I've been circling in my mind for months. I feel like such a dope."

The consultant responds, "Sure. You ask yourself something like, 'If I'm so smart, why am I so lost?'"

Here, the consultant places in front of Ben the assumption that is tacit in the words he has just spoken. That assumption seems to be as follows: smart people have sense made; I cannot make sense, so I must not be smart. Being smart and being in a state of no sense are incompatible given that assumption. Not until Ben sees this assumption and claims it as his own can he question and change it. Not until he changes it can he be his own advocate in making new sense of his life.

Replying to the consultant's question ("Sure. You ask yourself something like, 'If I'm so smart, why am I so lost?'"), Ben puts his feet down, emphatically, "Yeah. Right. Exactly!"

The consultant presses further in articulating what appears to be Ben's assumption: "Smart people don't get confused, right? And if they do, they figure their way out of there fast. And, if they can't be fast, at least they get it done alone, right?"

"I don't know. I guess so." Ben is ambivalent. Perhaps he is unsure if he wants to take full responsibility for his assumptions as stated by the consultant. He continues: "Do you think I'm dumb?"

He expresses the logical extension of his assumption: if smart is sense made and I cannot make sense, then I must be dumb.

"It's what you think of yourself that matters. You haven't answered my question."

"No, but . . ." Again Ben voices his ambivalence.

"You're neither here nor there?" asks the consultant, listening and legitimizing the ambivalence.

For the second time in this exchange, there is a pause of several seconds before Ben speaks. When he does, he asserts himself: "No, I'm not dumb. And I can't figure this out."

Ben sits upright, pulling his leg off the arm of the chair, placing his feet together on the floor, his change in posture mirroring the change in his tone from ambivalence to assertion. He has asserted a startlingly new relationship to his sense making: he is risking the radical possibility that what was wrong might be all right. Maybe smart and no sense can exist together. In this moment, he is to his new relationship to sense making as an explorer would be to arriving at a new land, at once excited and apprehensive.

The consultant cajoles, "A smart guy who can't make sense? Maybe these two things aren't mutually exclusive after all?"

"Maybe not," the young man says, smiling. He sits for a few moments and then continues: "But don't tell my dad."

The consultant laughs and asks, "You're ready to slosh around in this sorry condition of yours, are you?"

In joy and apprehension, Ben sits, smiling boyishly. At once acknowledging his new relationship to himself and seeking reassurance, he asks: "So I'm not stupid?"

Laughing, the consultant replies, "You can always make that choice!"

Ben begins to talk at length about the complexity of the study-test problem and its implications for his decision to drop out of college.

Commentary

Ben was in the grip of his reflexive relationship to sense making, as expressed by the question: "What's wrong with me that I am here?" Absent the invention of a reflective voice that can make new sense of his experience, he would remain focused on trying to get himself out of a bad place he felt he should not be in rather than exploring the nature of his study-test problem.

That he would have a reflexive relationship to his sense making is no mystery. The company we keep in the interpersonal world is the company we keep in our internal world. As the son grew up and risked revealing himself to be in "searching for sense" and "no sense," he heard his parents' voices spoken from the fix-it frame, offering fault-finding criticism and reassurance.

Fixed? No. Left in a fix—a debilitating internal conflict. When he is alone searching for sense or in no sense, he will advise himself as he was advised by his parents. He will fight the condition with self-criticism (for example, "Are you going to wallow in your own drivel?") or flee through reassurance (for example, "Maybe the course isn't worth taking in the first place"). As a result, he will be in limbo between being in no sense and struggling not to be, on the advice of his own internal voices. In effect, his energy and intellect would be knotted in an inner conflict. He needs to free them in order to focus on understanding the nature of the test conundrum.

Were the consultant to offer Ben fix-it criticism and reassurance, their interaction would simply mirror what's already going on in Ben's head, embedding him further in the internal conflict that leaves him stuck. Instead, the consultant relates to Ben reflectively. Through empathy, the consultant creates the opportunity for Ben to invent and choose a reflective way of relating to himself. The consultant creates conditions for invention (and discovery) by:

- Listening, trying to recognize and articulate Ben's struggle to extricate himself from no sense (hoping to legitimize where Ben finds himself, yet does not want to be). Until we feel an internal condition is legitimate, we cannot own it.

- Unearthing the reflexive assumptions about searching for sense and no sense, which are tacit in Ben's thinking (hoping to enable him to gain insight and commitment to his current assumptions, so that questioning them is possible). Until we see and commit to our current assumptions, however limited they may be, we cannot question them and discover their limits.

- Presenting reflective assumptions about the conditions of searching for sense and no sense (hoping to open the possibility that these conditions could be experienced as an internal resource rather than a liability). Until we have alternative assumptions, we cannot see and behave differently.

This combination of listening, examining embedded assumptions, and presenting alternative perspectives enables Ben to invent and choose a new way of thinking about his relationship to searching for sense and no sense, freeing him to focus on his test problem. The consultant behaves in these ways because he believes in a reflective rather than a reflexive model of human growth: reflectively, our model for growth is wholeness, where growth is an expression of learning to include all parts of the self to become whole.[1] Reflexively, our model for growth is perfection, where growth is an expression of learning to exclude parts of the self in order to be perfect.

In "So I'm Not Stupid?" Ben actively tries to get rid of parts of himself. His effort is to excise his no sense, using his most primitive, reflexive self: fight or flight:

- Fight: "Well, what's wrong with me?" he demands of the consultant, apparently expecting a quick fix.

- Flight: "Yeah, but how do I get out of this mess?" he asks the consultant, hoping to flee from his uncomfortable stuckness.

Tacitly, he is relating to himself through the common form of an if-then equation: If I can get rid of this unwanted presence (stuckness in this instance), then I can (feel, think, be better, do more or better). This if-then equation is the operational form of a perfection model of human growth. Like the son, we expect that people should be perfect.

The contrasting reflective assumption is that people yearn to be whole, though often expect to be perfect. When we act from our yearning to be whole instead of an expectation to be perfect, we assume that inclusion is the pathway to growth. So we work to welcome all of our different parts or voices into full participation within ourselves. This includes feelings, wishes, images, thoughts, and conditions such as searching for sense and no sense. The imperative for growth is this: if I can risk feeling my feelings or accepting myself as flawed, for example, then I can relate rationally and not defensively to others who present me with their feelings or flaws.

The very parts or voices we seek to welcome when inside a reflective model are those parts or voices we attempt to exclude within a reflexive model because the goal of growth is to be perfect, not whole. Our effort is to expunge unwanted parts or voices in pursuit of perfection. The imperative for growth is this: if I can get rid of my shortcomings and imperfections, for example, then I can be competent in whatever I do.

Internally, if we are trying to rid ourselves of our "bad" or "shouldn't be" parts, be they anger, fear, confusion, no sense, ambivalence, or uncertainty, then we will act interpersonally to rid other people of their "bad" parts, which we believe will keep them from attaining perfection.

In contrast, if we pursue becoming less fearful of our own fear, anger, or grief; more welcoming of the conditions of searching for sense or no sense; more aware and accepting of our yearnings to be taken care of, then we will be less likely to react with defensiveness when we are in the presence of others who are in fear, or no sense, or in need of help, just to give three examples. Unafraid of fear in ourselves, we no longer fear it in others. Accepting of the condition of no sense in ourselves, we can be accepting of it in others.

Story: Triumph at Work, Trouble at Home

To claim discrepancies as ours, we must invent a reflective voice within ourselves who can change fundamentally the nature of our internal dialogue, much like the voice of the consultant in "So I'm Not Stupid?" helped change Ben's internal dialogue. In effect, we must learn to relate reflectively to the defensive, reflexive part of ourselves. This is a prerequisite to nondefensive interactions with others; there is a direct correlation between the nature of the interaction in our heads and the interaction we can conduct in the interpersonal world.

In "Triumph at Work, Trouble at Home," we see a CEO/husband in the act of both discovering his own reflexive voice and inventing a reflective voice. The steps in inventing his reflective voice are:

1. Legitimizing his own internal experience

2. Relating to his reflexive voice reflectively

3. Consulting with his internal experience

In the end, he risks this journey to save his marriage. What he learns at home leads to changes in his leadership style at work. During the first year of his new CEO job, the man met every other week with an organizational consultant to design his entry into the organization. After three months, he began one of these consulting sessions by saying, "Triumph at work and trouble at home," continuing, "When I go home, my wife does nothing but moan." Asked what his wife said to him, he responded by offering her words in no particular order, though the first entry in the list confused him, and because she repeated it regularly, it caused him to raise the relationship issue with the consultant:

1. "I don't want you to problem-solve me; I want you to listen."

2. "My days are nothing but caretaking: you, the kids, the dog, the dishwasher, the washing machine that doesn't work. I don't like this house. Maybe I shouldn't be worried about money, but the other house isn't sold yet, so what do you expect?"

3. "Now this puppy! It's cutting right into my life: paper training, housebreaking, feeding, shots. I can't go out when I want to. The kids wanted the puppy, and I get the job of taking care of it. Believe me, I'm just going through the motions. God, what am I doing here?"

4. "I'm not too happy with you either. You get a life, and I get stuck in a house cleaning up dog puddles, fixing toilets, taxi-driving kids in a town I hate. I never wanted to move. Just like the last time, you at your cushy job and me picking up the pieces behind you!"

Asked what came to mind when his wife spoke in these ways, he predictably related judgmental thoughts about his wife:

1. In response to, "I don't want you to problem-solve me, I want you to listen," he felt unreasonably attacked. "What are you talking about? Listen? That's what I am doing. What do you want?"

2. In response to "My days are nothing but caretaking," he felt angry. "I'm working harder than ever! I would welcome the chance to trade places with you. These are small-time problems!"

3. In response to, "Now this puppy! It's cutting right into my life," he felt ambivalent. "The kids wanted the dog. I should have said no."

4. In response to, "I'm not too happy with you either," he felt cheated, resentful, and even frightened. "You never give me the chance to celebrate how well it's going at work. You're not going to threaten me again with this leaving stuff. I've got no choice but to overcommit at work, at least for now."

Asked what he actually said back to his wife, the husband related the two most recent examples of his predictable participation in the competition-for-listening pattern of interaction. It predicts that when we are given information (tacitly being asked to listen), we give information back (tacitly saying, "No, I cannot listen to you. I need you to listen to me"). Our focus here is on the husband's information-giving reaction to his wife:

Example One

Husband: It's great to see the kids so excited with the puppy.

Wife: The puppy! It's cutting right into my life. I can't go out when I want to with paper training, housebreaking, feeding, shots. The kids wanted the puppy, and I get the job of taking care of it. Believe me, I'm just going through the motions. God, what am I doing here?

Husband (gives information back): It's terrific what you are doing for the kids. It won't be long before they'll be able to help out more with the puppy. They're crazy about the little thing. Maybe we could send it somewhere to be trained.

Wife: You're a big help. Absent Mr. Fix-It!

Example Two

Husband: I had a great day today.

Wife (interrupting): If you'd been here, you'd be singing a different tune. My days are nothing but caretaking: you, the kids, the dog, the dishwasher, the washing machine that doesn't work. I don't like this house. Maybe I shouldn't be worried about money, but the other house isn't sold yet, so what do you expect?

Husband (gives information back): Look, there's no need for hand-wringing. They're short-term problems that we can solve.

Wife: Please don't treat me like a problem. I'm not a problem to solve. You can get by with that at work, but not with me!

These interactions continued in the competition-for-listening pattern, getting increasingly hostile, as had most of their attempts at conversation during his first three months on the new job. It is predictable. When the husband's wife gives him information he does not want to hear (negative information), he will react from a fix-it frame of reference, thinking something like, "What's wrong with her?" and blaming his wife in particular or himself. His judgmental thinking will shape his behavior into one of two corrective forms:

- Reassurance in the form of bucking up, encouraging, giving strokes, or cheering up, as in Example One

- Criticism, in the form of advice giving, information giving, straightening out, getting in line, or enlightening, as in Example Two

Because behavior follows from thinking, the husband cannot change his behavior to break the competition-for-listening pattern without changing his thinking. Before he could change his thinking, he needs to examine it in search of the embedded frame of reference. Since he believes his thinking is correct, it would be absurd to examine it. He is not the problem. His wife is the problem. She causes the competition-for-listening pattern. If he could get her to grow up, there would be triumph at work and triumph at home.

To be open or receptive to his wife's protestations that she feels treated like a problem to be solved, a wrong to be fixed, a deficiency to be remedied would make absolutely no sense to him. His behavior, which his wife experiences negatively, is a sensational success (we are talking about triumph at work here). She can say he only critiques or reassures, but he can give examples of variability in his repertoire. And if she is going to talk about the singularity of his responses, what about her always whining when the going gets tough? Is her worth in the marketplace seven figures a year? Does she deal successfully with hundreds of people a day? And, "If I only have this issue with her, isn't that evidence enough that *she* is the problem, not *me?*"

The emotional implications of "surrendering" the sense he has made of his strength and her weakness are enormous. Would he be a fraud? A fool? Stupid? Incompetent? Could he trust his judgment if he had been so blind? What might this say about his judgment in other situations? If it did raise doubt, how could he be so limited and yet so successful? The hint of such a cosmic discrepancy is experienced as at once absurd and terrifying.

These questions are the sloshing sound of sense-making soup. The husband did not like this sound in his own head and hated hearing it come from his mouth. It sounded like whining to him. So on the single occasion when he tried to talk with a friend about his trouble at home, he clammed up immediately.

Discovering His Reflexive Voice

What events, conditions, or forces could possibly compete against the gravitational pull of the sense he had made of his "wife as problem"? What creates receptivity to repelling information that promises to threaten the very ground we stand on? What could get the husband to engage in the process he considers "touchy-feely," the process of developing a new reflective, internal dialogue?

First, he was hounded by the fear of losing his second marriage, a possibility he escaped narrowly when he took a prior CEO position. Second, he was divided about taking on the challenge of living alone. "Do I want to buy my own toothpaste?" Third, he was haunted by the memory of his three grown children from his first marriage telling him that he had not "listened to mom." The consultant recommended that the husband speak to his grown children about how they had seen him relate to his first wife.

They told him that he had always treated their mom as a child. She had grown, they said, and he had not. He was stunned. The jolt allowed a whisper of possibility and then a wind of forceful disruption in the sense he had made of the situation.

Fourth, the organizational consultant with whom he was planning the entry into his new organization walked him through a self-reflective exercise, designed to help develop a new internal dialogue and then embody it in new interpersonal learning skills.

An Analytical Exercise

The exercise began with three activities, the results of which were reported to begin this story:[2]

- A list of the statements his wife actually made to him

- A list of his corresponding responses in feeling and thought

- Examples of how he expressed his feeling and thought in behavior

The consultant set up a fourth activity by asking the husband to entertain the possibility that his behavior and thinking followed from a fix-it frame of reference. He proposed to clarify this possibility by juxtaposing the fault-finding frame of reference with a sense-making frame of reference in a role-play activity, designed to show the relationships between frame of reference, thinking, and behavior.

The two men sat across from one another. The consultant, with a video camera beside him, role-played the husband's wife, using the material developed during the first activity. For example, he said to the husband: "I don't want you to problem-solve me, I want you to listen."

The husband's job was to listen to these words through the lenses of the following questions, attempting to find the question which revealed the sense his wife might be trying to convey:

Reflective Questions

- What feeling do I hear in her tone? And what seems to give rise to it?

- Is she expressing a tacit intent, hope, or fear?

- Does she have sense made? Is she trying to hand it over to me in the form of her successful theories, explanations, or reasons?

- Is she searching for new sense? Is she in the act of figuring, puzzling, analyzing, diagnosing?

- Might she be in a state of no sense? Could she be saying she is stuck, at the end of her rope, at her wits' end, not knowing which way to turn?

The crux of the effort for him was to put aside the questions and judgmental attributions that came to mind reflexively when he was confronted by his wife's words:

Reflexive Questions

- What's her problem?

- What's wrong now?

- What am I going to do about this?

When he was able to put aside briefly the reflexive questions he used automatically to hear his wife's words as complaining and instead process the same words through the reflective questions, he found the possibility of there being behind those words a person who wanted to be heard, where before there was only a problem to be solved. He found a wife who might be making sense of her life through the following feelings and thoughts: anger; fear of repeating the past (losing him to his job, of being abandoned again); hopeless and helpless about communicating with him, about his ever changing behavior, about ever feeling at home; trapped; isolated and alone with her anguish.

Perceiving his wife as a person with these feelings and thoughts left the husband ambivalent, at best.

"She could be an inveterate whiner, you know!" the husband exclaimed.

"Yes."

The husband went on, "You're saying she might not be? She might be a person who is feeling trapped and angry, and I don't perceive that because I'm looking at her through the dark glasses of a fix-it frame of reference?"

"Yes. And the only way to find out if she's an inveterate whiner or if you're blinded by your own frame of reference is for you to risk behaving differently with her so you can see what happens. Of course, you might be afraid to find out that you are wrong about her."

"Sure," the husband said. "Treat her like a person, not a problem, right? Well, I don't want to be the kind of person we created in this exercise!"

Inventing a Reflective Voice

Legitimizing His Own Internal Experience. The consultant urged the husband to reflect on how he related to the feelings, thoughts, and conditions within himself that his wife seemed to be expressing to him in their interactions. How did he treat himself when he found himself stuck, helpless, afraid, angry, anguished, or needy? Did he treat himself kindly, attempting to learn about and from these internal experiences? Or did he treat himself harshly in an effort to rid himself of them? If so, had he succeeded? If not, why not? Perhaps he was trying to expunge from himself (and his wife) experiences that were intangible yet normal, natural, and real. Was it possible that progress lay not in expelling these experiences but in welcoming them?

"This is alchemy?" asked the husband. "Weakness becomes strength!?"

"No," said the consultant, "but I do believe that strength follows from inclusion, not exclusion of the parts of ourselves we don't know much about and fear. Certainly inclusion is the source of interpersonal competence, let alone intimacy in relationships. How could you respond rationally to your wife if you reject the very parts of yourself that she expresses? If you reject fear in yourself as proof you're a 'weenie,' then you're bound by a sense of personal responsibility to rid her of fear. The thrust of your behavior will be to get her out of the fear she may be in, even though she may wish to be heard for who she is—simply a frightened person—not extricated from her fear by you."

By engaging with the consultant in self-exploration catalyzed by these kinds of questions, the husband inched toward a more knowledgeable and accepting relationship with his own whining voice, his own confusion, and the sense of helplessness and hopelessness he felt relative to his wife. Almost imperceptibly, he began to welcome the internal experience he had banished as traitorous. As he spent less energy banishing and more energy legitimizing the feelings and thoughts associated with his wife, he was able to explore the assumptions embedded in those thoughts and feelings.

Relating to His Reflexive Voice Metaphorically. The roots of a reflective voice grow in the soil of internal experience judged to be toxic by our reflexive voice. Until the husband even tentatively flirted with a choice to redefine and legitimize his fear, anger, confusion, and stuckness as related to his wife, he could not talk to himself differently enough to invent new behavior with his wife.

The limits of his reflexive thinking were self-evident to him as he role-played with the consultant and then watched the videotapes. When he thought (reacting to his wife's words, "I don't want you to problem-solve me, I want you to listen"), "What are you talking about? Listen? That's what I am doing," it was clear that this thinking could lead only to correcting his wife judgmentally.

Nevertheless, just because he could see the limits of this thinking, he wasn't about to give it up. It was him.

The consultant told him he didn't have to give up this reflexive thinking. In fact, he couldn't even if he wanted to. Alternatively, he could stop listening literally to it and start listening metaphorically to it as an expression of another feeling, intent, hope, thought, or condition in himself that he was less knowledgeable about and comfortable with. Operationally, he had to step back from the voice, almost as if he were listening to the words spoken by someone else and ask: "How am I feeling, or yearning, or what do I need, or what condition am I in when I talk to myself in this reflexive way?"

Though at first the consultant's request didn't make sense to the husband, it wasn't long before he blurted out, "When I can't instantaneously figure out what's going on, that's when I talk that way."

The husband was incredulous yet captured by his insight. After several weeks of reflection about its validity, he began to trust and use it as the knowledge he needed to create and practice a reflective dialogue with his reflexive voice when faced with the pressure of negative information from his wife.

Finding the words for his reflective voice to speak to his reflexive voice was a vexing problem. They could not be words of power. He could not tell his reflexive voice, "Shut up!" for example. The predictable consequence would be an internal competition for listening exchange, with each voice attempting to prevail over the other, the two voices egocentrically trapped in an internal conflict rather than focused on his wife.

The words he was looking for needed to express an understanding that the reflexive voice in all of us hopes to help us make sense and act effectively in the world. Understood in terms of its hope rather than its words, tone, or limitations, the reflexive voice can yield the floor of internal dialogue to a reflective voice of greater knowledge, kindness, firmness, and grace.

With the help of the consultant, the husband struggled to create a reflective statement he could believe in when he was under the pressure of a difficult interaction. What the two men came up with was: "I don't have to have sense made for myself before I try to understand and talk to my wife as a sense maker."

Choosing these apparently innocuous words is nothing less than making a commitment to welcome the banished (no sense, in this instance) into the fold. It is a choice to make the enemy kin. These words require a commitment to accepting the pain of his own no sense as legitimate, not toxic, not a deficiency — not a sign of incompetence or stupidity, for example. The interpersonal consequence of this dramatic redefinition is that he will not be compelled to rid himself of the pain of no sense, angrily throwing it at his wife in the form of blame, or "eating" it, reassuring her that everything is going to be all right.

The consultant juxtaposed an example of the husband's reflexive thinking with the proposed reflective response they had created. Reacting to his wife's words, "I don't want you to problem-solve me, I want you to listen," the husband thinks reflexively to himself, "What are you talking about? Listen? That's what I am doing." But then the husband would say in the silence of his own mind, "I'm having a difficult time making sense of what's going on. I don't have to have sense made for myself before I try to understand and talk to my wife as a sense maker instead of a problem to be solved."

It was not surprising that when the husband spoke the words of this new internal dialogue with himself, he felt uncomfortable, and why wouldn't he? He was verging on a profound redefinition of his internal world, attempting to surrender the miserable ease of treating himself as a problem (when in the condition of no sense) for the awkward vulnerability of empathy and compassion. Each attempt was a small step away from relating literally to the people-are-problems assumption as the solid ground of his being. Each step away was a step toward what appeared to be the quicksand of internal experience he'd spent his life avoiding.

Consulting with His Internal Experience. As his new conversation with himself became more inclusive of the personal experience he had long denied, energy he had been using to rid himself of his own experience was available to be directed toward learning about and from his internal experience and the interpersonal situation with his wife. For example, with his no sense available as a resource, he was able to ask himself questions such as:

- Does my no sense tell me about the limits of my frame of reference? She says I'm not listening. I think I am. So even though she's using the word *listening,* maybe she's asking for something I don't understand. Maybe I'm not listening in her terms.

- Does my no sense tell me that my wife is having difficulty making sense? Could I be having a sympathetic response, picking up what's going on inside her?

- Does my no sense tell me less about either one of us and more about the complexity of the subject between us?

Attempting New Behavior at Home

Over several months, practice sessions like those described helped the husband develop a new internal dialogue. That new dialogue enabled him to choose to behave differently when his wife gave him negative information, tacitly asking for him to listen.

When she said, again, "I don't want you to problem-solve me, I want you to listen," he heard his first reaction ("What are you talking about? Listen?! That's what I am doing.") as his reflexive voice, and he remembered that this was an expression of his inability to make sense instantly. Legitimizing his no sense, he said to himself, "I don't have to have sense made before I try to understand my wife as a sense maker." Then he chose to bring to mind a new question to make sense of his wife's words: "What is her tacit hope?" Reflecting on her words through this lens, he heard her plea not to be defined by him as defective. Hearing her hope, he said, "You want me to stop trying to fix you, to stop treating you as if you were a problem to be solved?"

There was a moment that neither of them will forget, for she felt known by him for the first time. She realized that he was capable of seeing the very blindness (to his own frame of reference) she despaired of his ever seeing. At the same time, she was uncertain and skeptical too, so she protected herself by saying, "So, you've been to charm school?"

He responded, "Yes. How am I doing?"

And she smiled: "Well, you're off to a promising start!"

The husband did not change the relationship with his wife through a single new response. As his wife said, though, it was a good beginning to a process of mutual learning that resulted gradually in payoffs at work as well as home. He is still married, and both he and his wife are pleased about that.

Exploring His Leadership Style at Work

Ten months into the CEO's new job and during the period of intense effort to change his behavior with his wife, the CEO lost two of his most valued executives to other companies. Their departures wounded him, as did the accompanying negative information from them about his leadership style.

Through exit interview information from the departing executives, he learned that a primary reason for their departures was a lack of opportunity for growth at the company. Both felt that as good as the CEO was in solving problems, he did not allow them to learn and develop. In the words of one executive, "I go to him, and he's got the answer, even for questions I haven't asked." In effect, the departing executives were saying that they had only competition for listening interactions with the CEO.

In an effort to explore the negative implications for his leadership style posed by the exit interview data, the CEO had the consultant interview each member of the remaining management team. To his astonishment, he discovered that his wife was not alone in how she felt on the receiving end of this behavior. In a few words, when the executives came to him not for his answers but for a sounding board, an expert listener, a guide, or a coach, they left with mixed feelings, impressed with his brilliance and yet empty, as if they did not exist in his presence.

Faced with this negative feedback, his initial bout of no sense was not nearly as painful as it had been when his wife gave him similar feedback. Through his wife's assertiveness in describing the effects of his behavior and his decision to engage anew with her, he had begun to invent a reflective dialogue with himself and an interactive leadership expressive of it. It was a leadership based not on having all of the answers himself but on asserting when he could not make sense and expecting others to join him in defining problems and solutions through interaction.

The elements of his emerging style are an expression of the values advocated in this book:

- Try to understand negative performance feedback that strikes the bone of your being rather than reflexively assuming the other person is up to no good.

- Seek understanding of other people's experiences and views rather than assuming that they need to be corrected.

- Examine your own behavior, thinking, and feeling as an integral part of team problem solving rather than analyzing the other persons' views only.

- Risk change in the very ground you stand on in an effort to move toward a new vision of productivity through teamwork rather than productivity through the competition-for-listening pattern.

A Final Note on the Process of Invention

To claim our participation in discrepancies, we must invent and learn to trust a reflective voice who can talk and listen to our reflexive voice as an equal in (rather than the ruler of) our internal dialogue. There is no guarantee that taking part in reflective, sense-making conversations will secure this result, let alone produce a new form of interpersonal learning based on trust engendered through disclosure, listening, and open agendas. However, taking part in reflexive, fix-it conversations will only reinforce the very reflexive interaction that is already going on inside our heads. That internal interaction represents itself in the world as the competition-for-listening pattern of interaction, resulting in mistrust and estrangement because of withholding, criticism or reassurance, and closed agendas.

The process of developing a reflective voice that we can choose instead of reacting from our reflexive voice is at once unnerving, chaotic, intimate, and immensely energizing. D. H. Lawrence captured the nature and quality of the process in *Studies in Classic American Literature*, when he compared the experience of such growth and change to that of a snake shedding its old skin:

> To slough the old consciousness completely, to grow a new skin underneath, a new form. This second is a hidden process. The two processes go on, of course, simultaneously. The slow forming of the new skin underneath is the slow sloughing of the old skin, and sometimes this immortal serpent feels very happy, feeling a new golden glow of a strangely-patterned skin envelop him: and sometimes he feels very sick . . . as he wrenches once more at his old skin, to get out of it. "Out! Out!" he cries, in all kinds of euphemisms. He's got to have his new skin on him before ever he can get out. And he's got to get out before his new skin can ever be his own skin. It needs a real desperate recklessness to burst your old skin at last. You simply don't care what happens to you, . . . so long as you do get out. It also needs a real belief in the new skin.[3]

The hard work of inventing your reflective voice and strengthening your confidence in its guidance will continue as you begin to practice the key skills of communicating to lead and learn.

Chapter Three

Practice: Getting Prepared

Discovery is about opening ourselves to our participation in discrepancies and realizing that our fix-it frame of reference accounts for them. A result can be motivation to invent a reflective voice to guide us in closing the gaps between how we aspire to interact with others and how we actually do. Here, we turn from a focus on the internal skills of discovery and invention. to practicing the interpersonal skills that express our insight into the limitations of our past practice and our commitment to a sense-making frame of reference that offers hope for making our behavior congruent with our aspirations.

Surely in turning from the internal world of changing our thinking to the external world of practicing new skills, our journey does not change from one kind of thing to another, as the distinction between focusing on thought first and then action might imply. In fact, at some point, taking new action becomes requisite to further discovery and invention. As we practice new interpersonal sense-making skills, we must expect to cycle back to discovery, gaining deeper insight into the nature of our reflexive frame of reference, and to invention, creating new, reflective perspectives that make interpersonal learning our priority.

There are three types of reflective, interpersonal, sense-making skills:

• Structuring

• Giving good information

• Listening (or getting good information)

These three skills are demonstrated as an integrated whole by Bill, the lead character from the story, "Are You Calling Me a Liar?" from Chapter One. Here we see a second, more skillful version of the story.[1] Then each skill is presented separately as a set of concepts and examples, along with the rationale for its use. "How To" sections for further study and reference are located in Chapter Five.

Story: Are You Calling Me a Liar? (Reflective Version)

The reflective version of this dialogue story clearly contrasts with the first (reflexive) version in demonstrating what it might look like to behave the way we like to think we behave: using open agendas (structuring for joint participation), giving good feedback, and listening for understanding.

Developing and using these skills would appear to be straightforward, but it is not. When we have something at stake, all of us naturally behave in opposition to these skills, and we are often unaware of it, as demonstrated in Bill's reflexive version handling of Mitch. Our patterns of natural, reflexive behavior are characterized by:

- Closed agendas: We structure to keep agendas closed by not revealing our real purposes and procedures (methods, tactics).

- Withholding information: We withhold observable data while revealing only our opinions or conclusions, and we tend to keep our sense making private rather than asserting it for inquiry.

- Criticism or reassurance: We criticize or reassure people when they present their side of things rather than listen.

Bill demonstrates the use of reflective, interpersonal sense-making behaviors that are necessary to close the skill gap and move from a reflexive to a reflective mode of communication:

- Open agendas: Structuring is jointly defining purposes, guidelines, and procedures so all parties in an interaction can know what's going on and why, and how to take part fully.

- Giving good information: Giving good information is picturing concretely for a person what we saw that person do that led us to a conclusion or opinion about the person's performance. In addition, it means asserting the thinking that accompanies our behavior, inviting feedback so we might gain insight into the embedded assumptions that drive our behavior. Finally, it means asserting explicitly the assumptions, perspectives, and values that underlie the use of interpersonal sense-making skills.

- Listening, or getting good information: Listening is striving to understand the other person's information, perspective, or experience and then testing that understanding out loud so the person can say yes, no, or modify what was originally said. The effort is not to assuage the other person but to gain knowledge through empathy, which might change our own ways of looking at things or enable the other person to do the same.

In short, the reflexive and reflective skill sets can be contrasted as shown at the top of the next page:

Reflexive	Reflective
Structure for closed agendas	Structure for open agendas
Withhold data	Give good data
Criticize or reassure	Listen for understanding

What might the Bill-Mitch interaction look like if Bill were able to enact the interpersonal learning skills shown on the right-hand side of the list?[2]

1. *Bill:* Come in, Mitch. Have a seat.

2. *Mitch:* Thanks. What's up?

3. *Bill:* I believe we have a problem.

4. *Mitch:* Oh? What is it?

5. *Bill:* I am not exactly sure, but I have been receiving some complaints from people who are unhappy about how they perceive you to be running the publications department.

6. *Mitch:* (interrupting) Who are they? What are they saying?

By trying to ease into the discussion with summary-type generalizations, Bill almost gets derailed before he is fully underway. He manages to hold Mitch's attention only by promising greater specificity and structuring the interaction.

Structuring

7. *Bill:* That's exactly what I asked you here to discuss. I'd like to tell you everything I've heard in as much detail as I can. After that, I'd like for you to tell me what you know about the situation. When we reach a common understanding about what the problem is, I want us to think about what we might do to solve it. I've got an hour on my calendar for this meeting, but if it appears that we need more time, we can schedule another meeting and continue later. How does all that sound to you?

Bill has proposed a structure for an interaction based on mutuality, that is, both persons knowledgeable about and in control of the agenda rather than unilateral control. He has suggested a purpose for the meeting (to investigate information reported to him by others and to develop a shared view of a problem), a procedure (alternating, bilateral disclosure), and a time period for the initial discussion. He also invites Mitch to approve or suggest changes in this structure.

8. *Mitch:* How does it sound? Like you're gonna dump on me, big time! Aren't you?

9. *Bill:* Yes, I guess so. I can only justify dumping this negative load by looking at the worse alternatives: instead of giving you the information, I could keep it to myself and make decisions about you and your future without your input. You'd be in the dark, with no opportunity to influence your own future.

   Or I could give you one piece of information at a time. We'd argue about every piece, one after the next: Who said this? How can you be so sure of that? You'd be kept off guard by not knowing how many items of bad news I plan to pull out of my bag. I'd be feeling that we were missing the point. Key parts of the information are interrelated and add up to something more than we can get at by debating each part. These are worse alternatives, don't you think?

10. *Mitch:* So are you firing me?

11. *Bill:* No. I'm trying to include you in figuring out what's going on, so I can make an informed decision about what needs to be done.

12. *Mitch:* Well, what's this all about then?

13. *Bill:* All right. There are five recent incidents related to past patterns of behavior as reported to me by your two past supervisors. I'll start with the recent incidents that seem to illustrate the patterns identified in the past.

14. *Mitch:* What?! You've been talking to those guys? This is a lynching!

15. *Bill:* No, it isn't. If anything, I'm attempting to make this the opposite of a lynching. Until you know what I know, and I know your information, we can't figure out together what's going on here. I'll tell you what they said, then I want your reaction. But I'm going to begin with the recent incidents.

Giving Good Data About Observation and Related Inference

16. *Bill:* First, I've heard from the marketing manager and sales manager that the publications department did not meet printing deadlines for important brochures they ordered a few weeks ago.

17. *Mitch:* That's not true!

18. *Bill:* Mitch, let me run through all of this at least once, and then we can back up and you can tell me anything you think is important. Will you let me do that?

19. *Mitch:* Well, okay, but I want you to know that we meet our deadlines!

20. *Bill:* Okay. My second area of concern is that your secretary and the printing staff tell me that one reason those two brochures were late is that you pushed those jobs aside to make way for a job from the CFO.

21. *Mitch:* Squealers! What do they know!

22. *Bill:* Please, Mitch, let me finish. Third, some staff members say that when they raised questions about that particular change in the printing schedule, you got angry and yelled at them to "shut up" and "mind their own business."

    Fourth, your secretary tells me that when the marketing and sales managers came to ask about their work, she heard you tell them that their jobs were late because the press operators had "screwed up" and the jobs would have to be redone—and not because you yourself bumped their jobs to the end of the line.

    Fifth, I asked you again last week for a copy of the publications fee schedule, and you said you would send it to me right away. When I didn't get it, I asked your secretary for a copy, but she said she doesn't know anything about a fee schedule. She says she has no idea where the prices come from on the bills you have her send to customers.

    Finally, the reports of these incidents led me to contact your two prior bosses to find out if they were familiar with what I was hearing. Were these single incidents or examples of patterns of behavior over time? Both of them said they suspected you of playing favorites in print job pricing and scheduling and that you blamed production problems on the printers when the problems resulted from your own decisions. Though there is nothing in writing, they both say they spoke to you about these conclusions, and you denied them.

Bill now moves from disclosure of his observations and those of others into a disclosure of his own feelings about the data and its tentative meaning and implications for him.

    Based on what I've heard, I am concerned about our customers' confidence in the publications department. I am worried that some of them have reason to doubt that their work will be delivered on time at costs they feel are fair and consistent. It appears to me that the continuing lack of a published fee schedule suggests to customers that your pricing may be arbitrary and that you may play favorites with some customers. I'm worried that some customers may doubt that you are telling them the truth at all times.

    I'm also worried about overall morale in the department. It appears to me that your staff is nervous and unhappy, and I believe that bad morale will almost certainly affect productivity down the road. And I'm worried about you too. It is clear to me that you are a superb graphic artist, but what this all means to me is that you may be having trouble managing the overall publications operation.

23. *Mitch:* Is that all?

24. *Bill:* Yes. Except to say that the people who spoke to me allowed me to use their names because they want to improve things for themselves, for you, and your clients. They are not out to get you, nor am I. Their worst fear is that you will hear this information only as stabbing you in the back and seek retribution. They want you to know that they turned to me out of desperation; they could not get your ear in their efforts to help.

Listening

25. *Mitch:* I can't believe you went behind my back to talk to my staff like this!

Bill could choose to respond accusingly to Mitch's defensiveness (e.g., "Do you have something to hide, Mitch?"). Instead, Bill inquires, seeking to identify and give voice not just to Mitch's words but to what the meaning seems to be to him of those words.

26. *Bill:* It was undermining for me to talk directly with your staff?

27. *Mitch:* You bet it was! Yes, it was!

Mitch confirms wholeheartedly what Bill had inferred. The urgency in Mitch's tone arouses Bill's senses to what the "undermining" might mean to Mitch: lack of trust. So he listens by testing this inference.

28. *Bill:* Trust. Is that what's at stake?

29. *Mitch:* It's perfectly obvious that you don't trust me!

Giving Good Data About Observation and Related Inference

30. *Bill:* Mitch, I'm afraid that's somewhat true. I don't trust you altogether, because from nearly the moment I came here, I started hearing complaints about how you run the publications department.

When Mitch confirms that the issue is trust, Bill embraces the opportunity to disclose that he does have trouble trusting Mitch. Ironically, this admission could provide evidence that Mitch can trust what Bill says.

31. *Mitch:* Well, that's just dandy! Why didn't you come to me from the beginning? If you cared about hearing my side of the story, all you had to do was ask. Why didn't you give me a chance?

32. *Bill:* I should've talked with you about specific issues as they came up. Unfortunately, I avoided dealing with unpleasant information.

33. *Mitch:* You better believe it!

34. *Bill:* I'm trying to address these issues now. I do want to give you a chance. That's why I am more than eager to hear what you have to say about the information I have just shared with you.

Bill has taken responsibility for his own shortcomings as Mitch's supervisor. If he doesn't, how can he expect Mitch to do the same with his job?

35. *Mitch:* Well, you really dumped on me. I hardly know where to begin.

36. *Bill:* It's important that we talk through all of this information, but I think you can start anywhere you want.

Listening

37. *Mitch:* Okay. I admit I yelled at the print shop staff the other day, okay? But I think I was justified. Sometimes you just can't get printers to shut up and do their work. They ask too many questions. They don't want to do what I tell them to do.

38. *Bill:* And that makes you frustrated and angry?

Again, Bill is listening in the sense of paying attention not just to Mitch's words but to the tone in which Mitch speaks them. By acknowledging Mitch's obvious pain and anger, Bill shows his commitment to understanding Mitch's experience and perspective.

39. *Mitch:* That's right. I just blow up! They have to know who's in charge!

40. *Bill:* You figure that if you show your anger, they will follow your instructions with fewer questions?

Bill actively inquires to understand the apparent intent of Mitch's behavior, as Mitch experienced it.

41. *Mitch:* Yes! That's what it seems to take to get them to do their work.

42. *Bill:* Your yelling is a last-ditch attempt to motivate the printers?

43. *Mitch:* (interrupting) Yes. If they would just do what I say the first time, we could get everybody's work done on time, and nobody would be unhappy.

44. *Bill:* So here is how I am making sense of this. Your goal is to please people by being efficient and on time with what you promise. If the printers followed your orders immediately, you would meet this goal. But they don't. In frustration, you yell at them to motivate them to quicken their pace of work. But that doesn't work all the time either?

45. *Mitch:* Yeah, yeah. (pause) That's it. Are you saying I'm blaming the printers?

46. *Bill:* Actually, I was trying to reconstruct my understanding of how you see the situation. How am I doing?

47. *Mitch:* They can be real jerks. (pause) But it's not all their fault that we miss deadlines once in a while.

By listening past Mitch's words to the possible meaning in tone and tacit intent and then telling back to Mitch his own version of events, Bill has helped Mitch reflect on and articulate for himself what could be new knowledge about the nature of a problem of missing deadlines that earlier he denied existed: Mitch seems to have recognized that he is blaming the printers and has explicitly said there are other causes for missed deadlines. For now, Bill does not focus on the limits of Mitch's repertoire for motivating the printers or alternative causes of missing deadlines. Conscious of the time and wanting to review all of his data with Mitch, Bill turns again to the specific data he relayed at the beginning of the conversation.

Structuring

48. *Bill:* Mitch, I'll come back to this topic of your relationship with the printers and other possible causes for missing deadlines. Right now, I want to make sure we explore all of the areas of information I put in front of you. So a few days ago, there was an incident involving a request from the CFO.

Listening

49. *Mitch:* The CFO came to me with a big printing job he needed done at the last minute. I knew we already had the marketing and sales jobs scheduled, but he's the CFO! What am I supposed to do? Ignore him?

50. *Bill:* So you told the printers to put that job ahead of the others because you felt you had to obey the wishes of the CFO?

51. *Mitch:* That's right. I knew it might make the other jobs late, but I didn't have a choice.

52. *Bill:* Did you tell the CFO that other people's work might be late if you moved his work to the front of the line?

53. *Mitch:* Well, I tried to say something, but I knew he was in a hurry. He said he needed his handbooks right away.

54. *Bill:* What exactly did you say to him to explain your situation?

55. *Mitch:* Well . . . nothing, I guess. I *wanted* to. But I just *couldn't.*

56. *Bill:* You wanted to say something, but you were afraid?

57. *Mitch:* Yeah, I didn't know how to tell him.

Bill now understands Mitch's motivation for scrambling the printing schedule. However, at this point, Bill's secretary interrupts to tell him that the CEO's office has called and Bill is needed there immediately.

Structuring

58. *Bill:* Mitch, I think we're on to something potentially useful here. It appears that this latest change in the printing schedule was caused by your decision to accommodate the CFO, not by the printers. Right?

59. *Mitch:* Yeah, yeah. It was for the most part.

60. *Bill:* I think we have a lot more talking to do, but before we can do that, I have to run next door. If the CEO needs me for just a second, we can continue this conversation right away. If it looks as if I'll have to stay for a while, I'll come back to you long enough to schedule another meeting for today or tomorrow. Please wait for just a minute while I find out.

61. *Mitch:* All right.

Bill leaves and returns a few minutes later and explains that he must go to a meeting with the CEO. He schedules a time to continue this meeting with Mitch.

62. *Bill:* Mitch, I'm sorry about stopping in the middle of this. Given the mistrust between us, it's lousy timing for me to ask for a commitment from you. But here goes. I hope you won't speak to members of your department about this meeting. I have caught you off guard with a load of negative information, so you would naturally feel undermined, mistrusted, even betrayed by me and the people in your department who spoke to me. It would be understandable if you hear my request as further evidence of a conspiracy against you.

    I'm not conspiring with your department. I'm not blaming you totally for what's going on. Your department members are not out to get you. I'm trying to get in a position to understand what's going on and be helpful to you and your department. I worry that if you speak to department members, you will only make matters worse now.

    I can help you build trust with them so they come to you and not to me. I want to do that.

63. *Mitch:* I'm not sure what to say.

64. *Bill:* Can I count on you to handle this information alone until we meet again tomorrow?

65. *Mitch:* I don't know. I guess so.

66. *Bill:* You're unsure?

67. *Mitch:* No. Okay.

Commentary

If you refer back to the reflexive version of this interaction in Chapter One, you can recall how the conflict escalated. Here, Bill uses the three reflective skills to move the interaction and the relationship toward mutual understanding and hope for change. Where he was previously "talking tough," here he is "talking sense," with a much more positive outcome.

Yet this version of the story may provoke a "Yes, but" reaction: skepticism about various issues from whether Bill really accomplishes anything here to the formulaic quality of his use of the skills. If your skepticism is aroused, you might go immediately to Chapter Five and its sections on practice and action, where skeptical questions about reflective practice are asked and answered. Or you might be encouraged to hold your skepticism in abeyance and read on by entertaining this idea: as we read, our minds often leap out from the text to a difficult relationship in our own lives. Picturing the other person in the relationship, we attempt to fit our analysis of a character's use of a skill to an interaction with the person from our real lives. Scenarios run through our minds. In effect, we are making applications of the skill, and, based on what we imagine in our scenarios, we make judgments about whether the skill can be applied. If the application is not credible, we say, "It doesn't work; it's not worth learning."

It is useful to remember here that we can see the downside of anything strange more easily than the downside of the familiar. The downside risks of entertaining reflective practice are easy to enumerate. The downside risks of our reflexive mode of interaction are less easy to see but arguably much higher. The suggestion here is that you temporarily separate the learning of these skills from applying them and deciding their worth. When we can actually produce a skill repeatedly, as contrasted with thinking about producing it (closing the skill gap we discovered earlier), our perspective on how to apply the skill and how valuable it is can change dramatically.

The Structuring Skill: Concepts, Examples, and Rationale

Structuring, or setting the boundary conditions for an interaction, makes it possible for two or more people to work together (making new sense, as opposed to correcting or protecting) through disclosure of information and listening for understanding. Structuring can and should occur at three points during an interaction: the beginning, middle, and end.

Structuring is not simply a behavior but rather a careful framing of the following three analytical questions:

- What is the purpose of the interaction?

- What is the procedure for the interaction?

- What is the time period for the interaction?[3]

Metaphorically, structuring lets people clarify the rules before trying to play the game of joint problem solving. They do this by jointly setting the boundary definitions for the interaction: the purpose, procedure, and time period.

Typically, the person structuring an interaction would present this structure as a draft, not a finished product. The draft may or may not be adequate to the needs of both parties at the outset. If not, revise it. You say in tone if not words: "Here is my draft purpose and plan of action. I want your feedback. We can revise it. It needs to be a plan that makes sense to both of us."

Structuring to Begin an Interaction

Prior to an interaction, you need to make sure that all three central aspects of reflective structuring (purpose, procedure, and time period) are clear to all parties in the interaction. Each of these is a boundary condition: defining what is targeted (as opposed to what is not), defining a set of steps to guide working together (as opposed to other possible steps), and defining an amount of time.

Reflexively, we tend to keep information about our real purpose, procedure, and timetable in our minds rather than presenting it to the other person early and then inviting discussion and revision. By withholding this information, we reflexively act on the truism that information is power and keep unilateral control of the interaction. The other person, in the dark about what is really going on, wonders: "Why am I here, really? Where is this headed? How long will this take?" These private questions arise from feelings of vulnerability, anxiety, and mistrust, all of which contribute to the other person's responding defensively and reacting in a way that contributes to the competition-for-listening pattern.

Therefore, to ensure that all parties clearly understand the structure of an interaction, we need to ask five questions before beginning an interaction.

1. *Purpose:* What is my real purpose? What outcome am I after? If, having identified my real purpose, I cannot imagine saying it explicitly to the other person, then I am probably stuck in a reflexive mode of thinking and am likely to behave reflexively.

2. *Procedure:* By what steps do I see myself getting from here to there? Or what is my procedure for us working together?

3. *Time period:* How long do I see this meeting taking?

4. *Test and revision:* Can I present the information about purpose, procedure, and time period early in the interaction, discuss it with the other person, revise my plans as appropriate, and then use the structure to guide our efforts?

5. *Maximizing opportunity for choice:* Can I invite the other person's input, giving him or her some choices about how to proceed?

The tough meetings to structure are those requiring us to give negative information: information that the other person would not want to hear and that we would rather not give. A useful example of good structuring for meetings of this kind is the following: "I'd like to tell you everything I know about X incident, ask you to tell me what you know, and finally, I want us to work together to come up with a resolution within the next half hour. If we need more time, we can schedule it after three o'clock today. What do you think about this way of proceeding?" If the other person says, "Sounds good to me," the speaker would continue, "How would you like to begin? Do you want me to go first, or would you prefer to start?" This can be broken down for analysis in this way:

Purpose: We want to come to resolution regarding X.

Procedure: (1) I tell all; (2) you tell; (3) we resolve X.

Time period: One-half hour.

Test and revision (if necessary): "What do you think about this way of proceeding?"

Maximizing opportunity for choice: Give the other person the choice about who should begin.

The operating principle here is that it takes reflective structuring to create the conditions for mutuality in talk and listening. In contrast, reflexive structuring creates the conditions for the competition for listening. The construct can be observed in the following example, written by a school principal. The principal does not begin by clarifying purpose, procedure, or time frame and consequently contributes to creating the competition-for-listening pattern of interaction:

Principal: Charlene, I'd like to speak with you if you have a few minutes. This year, you've had trouble two or three times getting grades on the report cards on time.

Charlene: Only twice this year.

Principal: It's a real holdup for others, and it's important. And there's another problem. Last week, I had to cover your class because you were late to school. I'd have talked to you about it then, but there was that upset with those two girls. I want to see an improvement.

Charlene: (interrupting) I've only been late twice this year! And what's the big deal anyway? Why aren't we talking about the quality of my teaching?

Principal: Why aren't you getting your papers back to students on time? Why aren't you getting your grade cards in on time? You know we've talked about these problems before, and nothing's changed. And you continue to be late to class. I've had to cover your class more than twice, and I've spoken to you about it too, repeatedly.

Charlene: (interrupting) Now that really bothers me. I know I've only been late twice. There was the car accident, and this last time . . .

Principal: reaching for her calendar log and flipping through) Let's see, December 18, that was the accident. October 11, you broke your toe. November 13, heavy traffic. November 29, car trouble.

Charlene: (interrupting) I've had a lot of car trouble this year.

Principal: (still flipping through the log) I've only looked back quickly. Next year I want to see an improvement.

Charlene: (interrupting) I've had a lot of car trouble.

Principal: Perhaps you should leave for school earlier. You must improve!

Instead, the principal might have begun the interaction in a reflective manner as follows, attempting to clarify purpose, procedure, and time period:

> Charlene, during this year we've met *X* times and discussed two problems with your performance that upset me: your failure to return papers to students promptly and your getting report cards in late. Today I want to return to these two problems and, in addition, focus on a third, similar problem of lateness: you have been coming late to class. I have asked for this meeting so the two of us can plan how you will stop being late with papers, reports, and to class.
>
> Before getting into the specifics of my concern, I want to emphasize that I am not calling into question your overall performance as a classroom teacher. You are a fine teacher. Let's begin by clarifying what the facts are concerning your pattern of lateness. Then we can discuss the consequences to others of the pattern of lateness. Finally, we can work together to develop a plan for changing the pattern next year. I've set aside an hour now, and if we need more time, I will find it. Is this agenda clear and does it make sense?

The interaction would continue with the principal and teacher clarifying the facts about lateness and the consequences of lateness to others. Then they would develop and write a plan for changing the pattern of lateness.

In this example, the principal initiated the interaction. But had Charlene initiated instead, the principal still could have structured reflectively. However, when someone else initiates (for example, a colleague, employee, student, or child who comes seeking our help), we tend to respond reflexively by asking Twenty Questions, that is, one discrete question after another. Of course, the name "Twenty Questions" is not meant to be literal but rather to call to mind a pattern of behavior in which only the question asker, not the receiver, knows what the next question will be.

The following interchange illustrates the difference between reflexive Twenty Questions and reflective structuring when someone else initiates the interaction. A supervisor comes to a manager, saying, "We need to talk about what to do with Bob Bond. He talks incessantly in my staff meetings! My attempts to correct the situation haven't worked." The manager does not begin by clarifying the purpose, procedure, and time frame for the interaction. Instead, in knee-jerk fashion, the manager structures the interaction using the Twenty Questions approach:

> "What have you tried?"

"You name it, I've tried it!"

"Have you talked to him?"

"Yeah. Didn't do any good."

"Are other people complaining?"

"Yeah."

"Does he refuse to yield the floor, or what?"

"Yes. That's part of it. He interrupts. He keeps going after the ending time."

"Why does he do this?"

"Your guess is as good as mine."

"Is he a troublemaker?"

"He's a pain, yeah, most of the time."

"Most of the time?"

"He's got his good points."

"What are they?"

Twenty Questions is a reflexive, one up–one down form of structuring. Only the question asker knows what question comes next. The receiver has to guess, and does, thereby becoming split inside. A person who is split inside is in emotional limbo—neither here nor there, feeling vulnerable and perhaps mistrusting. Thus, although the manager may be well intentioned, the supervisor in the example could easily feel cross-examined rather than helped.

To avoid putting the supervisor in a one-down position at the outset, the manager needs to structure the interaction reflectively to create a "work with you" rather than a "work on you" pattern of exchange. For example, the manager might have said: "Why don't we try to reconstruct what you've done to solve this problem. When we've reconstructed your efforts, let's stop and analyze why they haven't worked. Then we'll figure out something to try next. What do you think?" The manager would then modify the sequence in response to the supervisor's feedback and use the revised structure to guide joint inquiry.

This reflective approach increases the likelihood of a partnership in the interaction. Both the manager and the supervisor can use the same set of problem-solving steps to arrive at an agreed-on objective. In contrast, a reflexive, Twenty Questions approach keeps the manager alone in control of the rules of the game.

There are added advantages to structuring reflectively. Because the problem-solving methodology is explicit between the two parties, both can suggest changing it if it isn't working. Two people identifying and making adjustments in the process are more likely to find and correct errors than one. Also, if the problem-solving methodology is explicit and shared, the manager and supervisor can return to it, evaluate it, and revise it after using it to address the immediate problem. Reflective structuring aims to make communication an act of interpersonal learning where participants examine, change, and improve their own practice.

Structuring in the Middle of an Interaction

You may also need to step back and structure periodically during an interaction. For example, two managers are at each other's throats, locked in a typical, escalating competition-for-listening pattern. They are making serious threats at one another, Manager 1 having requested a change of some kind for Manager 2:

Manager 1: So you're covering up a problem the IFO [a regulatory agency] should know about. I'll tell the IFO what you are doing. They'll get you for it!

Manager 2: Go ahead. You'll only embarrass yourself and your organization!

Manager 1: You'll probably lose your job when the facts are known.

Typically, the interaction might continue in this accusatory fashion and end in disaster for both men. But fortunately, Manager 2 realizes that they are in trouble and tries to restructure the interaction from a reflexive, competition-for-listening pattern to a reflective inquiry by saying: "We're not hearing one another, are we? Isn't this just a verbal battle? Let me try to state your position; then you listen to mine. Is that okay?"

In effect, Manager 2 is trying to construct a new boundary condition. He rules out of bounds reflexive, accusatory information giving and rules in bounds listening to one another's different positions. As well, he is suggesting a set of procedural steps to follow:

1. (Tacit) You state your position.
2. I'll try to state your position back to you.
3. I'll state my position.
4. You'll state my position back to me.
5. (Tacit) Then we'll see where we are, trying to make our way out of this accusatory trap we're in.

Manager 1 says, "Fine." Then, inside this new structure, the exchange is transformed, as evident in the following exchanges:

Manager 2: You think there is no link between the prior manager's request and your own, so I should have served your need for a change immediately. Your need is urgent. You don't trust my assumption about a link, so I seem to have gone out of my way to protect myself somehow and to inconvenience you?

Manager 1: Exactly.

Manager 2: I understand your position now. I think your request and the former manager's request are linked. If I approve your request, then his inaction will have to be reported to the IFO, even though we have not done anything wrong or illegal. If you do the paperwork to withdraw the original request, then resubmit yours, I can approve yours; then you can take action and report the closure without threat of sanction for the prior inaction.

Manager 1: So you were trying to keep us from getting unnecessarily embarrassed by the IFO?

Manager 2: Exactly.

At this point, the two managers have broken the competition-for-listening pattern. They have used their reflective structure to create a space for giving good information and listening. With a shared understanding of one another's views, they have set the stage for inventing together a mutually satisfying resolution to the confrontation.

Structuring to Close an Interaction

Structuring the beginning and middle of an interaction makes it more likely that the two parties can build mutual understanding and agreements. Structuring the close of an interaction helps ensure that those mutual understandings and agreements are acted on. By answering the questions, "Who does what with whom, when, and where?" structuring gets in place an agreed-on set of steps about what actions (if any) to take, or about how to guide further inquiry. For example, continuing the interaction between Manager 1 and Manager 2, a reflective close might look like this:

Manager 1: I'm now clear on why you did it. But we need the change as soon as possible.

Manager 2: Before you leave here, I'll put in your hands the paperwork you need to withdraw the prior request. Get it to me today? Today I'll confer with my investigator, you with your supervisors. You find out from them the date you can begin work with my investigator. Let's talk before 6:00 P.M., when we'll settle on the date and the timing of your resubmitting your new request for a change. When I get it, I'll approve it. Sound okay?

Manager 1: Yes, that's okay. I've got to write a few notes. I'm glad we discussed this. It prevented a serious misunderstanding.

Manager 2 takes the lead in structuring for effective closure by articulating the meeting of minds in operational terms, rather than reflexively closing the interaction by simply saying, "Okay, I'll get it done," and walking out. In fact, "getting it done" seems to involve a number of interrelated steps that require initiative on the part of both mangers. By defining those steps and checking out whether Manager 2 agrees, Manager 1 increases the likelihood that their breakthrough in reflective communication will result in a problem effectively solved.

Yes, But: Structuring Skill

We tend to prefer informal interactions and balk at structuring as too formal.[4] To imagine structuring an interaction is to hear ourselves getting dissed. Why would we make ourselves the object of ridicule? Surely structuring will inhibit exchange, not enable it.

For example, everyone gets anxious about structuring to begin a group meeting: "Before we begin, let's define our hoped-for outcome, how we'll proceed, and how long we'll stay at this topic before stopping." Surely, a participant will say, "Aw, c'mon, we're not going to sit around and talk about what to talk about are we? Let's get to it!"

Such a possible challenge evokes fear in the form of, "What will I say back?" Fear of appearing too formal and fear of not knowing how to respond to a challenge are both potential emotional barriers to structuring.

For the most part, our reflexive way of structuring is to keep control of the agenda by withholding our real purpose and plans for achieving it. So by contrast alone, the reflective idea of sharing our agenda and perhaps revising it through interaction can sound like "being conciliatory and weak" instead of "assertive and strong." We fear giving away the store, right from the outset.

Why Use the Structuring Skill?

As we have seen from the examples, reflexive structuring keeps the problem solver as the only active participant in an exchange. The problem solver collects data, then privately analyzes the problem, invents possible solutions, and offers them for use. Reflexive structuring errs by positioning the problem solver to do all of the following:

- To make critical or reassuring statements (see the Charlene example above and the parents' responses to the son in "A Son Drops Out of College") or ask a series of discrete questions to get information (see the Twenty Questions example above)

- To analyze privately the information received from the other person

- To produce a solution privately

- To offer it for use by the other person

In contrast, reflective structuring turns this private process inside out by positioning all parties, as active learners in an interaction, to do all of the following:

- To establish clear and shared purpose, procedure, and time period

- To share information

- To analyze the information and definition of the problem jointly

- To jointly invent possible solutions and next steps

Operating inside a reflexive structure, the problem solver's analytical and problem-solving forms, as well as sense-making processes and criteria for making judgments, remain largely private. Lacking access to the private processing, the receiver can neither take full part in the interaction nor learn how to become a more able learner and problem solver.

Operating inside a reflective structure, the problem solver makes public the previously privately held analytical or problem-solving forms, methodologies for joint inquiry into complex data, and criteria for making judgments. Thus, all people in the interaction can learn about and use these tools. The product of such an interaction is not only a solution to a particular problem but also increased shared knowledge about the methods and tools of joint problem solving.

The Skill of Giving Good Information: Concepts, Examples, and Rationale

Giving good information means breaking the habit of giving reflexive, judgmental information that is only inferential and often accusatory, and instead, giving observable data along with the related inferences drawn from it. It means breaking the habit of keeping our sense making private, and instead opening up our sense-making process to others and inviting them to join us in a search for new sense. Such interactions express an ethic of communication as interpersonal learning.

Giving good data means explicitly talking about this ethic in the form of reflective assumptions, perspectives, and values. We do not simply talk about the principles in the abstract; rather, we speak about them during conversations when we are using learning skills. We want to make self-evident what we are doing and why, in the hope that others might join us in mutual inquiry.

There are three forms of giving good information:

1. Disclosing our observational data as well as our inferences

2. Asserting our search for sense

3. Asserting reflective assumptions, perspectives, and values

Disclosing Our Observational Data as Well as Our Inferences

How we give information can influence whether the receiver feels blamed and simply blames in return, or feels informed and open to inquiry.

When giving information, the reflective principle is to give good information to get good information. In part, this means presenting observational data (specific, concrete, quantitative data) distinguished from the sense we make of these data. This isn't natural. Impulsively, we say to our son, "If you leave that bathroom messy one more time, there's going to be trouble!" But the word *messy* is a judgmental inference given without the observational information that led us to it. In fact, there is a good chance that our son does not entirely understand what we mean by "messy" even though we are angry that he is not seeing what is so obvious to us.

Such judgmental behavior follows directly from thinking, "How am I going to get my son to behave correctly?" At a deeper level, it follows from the reflexive frame of reference: fix it! When we act from this reflexive frame of reference, judgmentally accusing our son of wrongdoing, we are partly responsible for his angry, judgmental response: "Get off my back, will ya, Mr. Clean!"

Alternatively, we can choose to think and act from a different frame of reference: Where am I in my sense making? We make sense by observing the world and drawing inferences in thought and feeling. Knowing this, we can construct an initial statement that will more likely be received as information rather than accusation.

A popular form of giving good reflective data is I-statements or "When, I feel, because."[5] By presenting data in the form of an I-statement, we avoid the reflexive error of presenting our inferences without the observational information from which we drew them. For example, we ask our son to come into the bathroom and give him specific, concrete, quantitative information about what we find troubling.

When: "I see your washcloth, soap, and hair in the tub, clogging the drain. The showerhead is dripping. Over here, your dirty socks and your underwear are in the wastebasket with the wet towel. In the washbasin there are three gobs of toothpaste along with the cap."

I feel: "I am angry."

Because: "Because it takes me twenty minutes to clean up and feel comfortable using this place. As a result, I'm running late to work."

Here, we have taken the judgmental inference "messy" and broken it into its component parts of observations (when . . .), feeling meaning (I feel . . .), and impact (because . . .). Our frame of reference is not one of fault finding and fixing. Instead, the frame is one of sense making: "Here are my observations and related inferences. What is your information, or what do you make of mine?" Minimally, acting from this less judgmental frame of reference evokes less defensiveness in the listener. Our son can see what we saw and how it affected us rather than feel accused of wrongdoing. In return, he can offer better data to us in the same mode of sharing observations rather than judgmental statements. And, as it is for him, so it is for us. If he uses an I-statement, we can then see what he saw and make sense of his inferences rather than react reflexively to them as wrongs we need to set right. As a consequence, we are less likely to react defensively when he responds.

The following examples further illustrate the difference between giving information reflexively (inferences in the form of judgmental statements, without the observations which led to them) and giving information reflectively (specific, concrete, quantifiable observations, separated from feeling and impact):

Giving Data, Example One

Context: I tell a colleague that I'm upset that she implied I was negligent in not getting a project to her on time when, in fact, she set no deadline date.

Typical reflexive, judgmental way of giving of information: "There was no reason for you to talk to me that way this afternoon!"

Reflective way of giving information: Observations (facts) and inferences: "This afternoon, when you said to me, 'I expected you to get me that memo last week at the very latest!' I was caught off guard and upset because I had every intention to write it but was not aware that you needed it so soon."

Giving Data, Example Two

Context: I tell a new employee that I was disturbed with his joking and interrupting in the last staff meeting I ran.

Typical reflexive, judgmental way of giving of information: "What did you think you were doing in that meeting today, fooling around like that?"

Reflective way of giving information: Observations (facts) and inferences: "Today in the staff meeting, you joked and interrupted. I was upset because I could not get through the last three items on my agenda."

Giving Data, Example Three

Context: I call a supervisor in to discuss his performance in handling tardy employees.

Typical reflexive, judgmental way of giving of information: "You're not running a hair salon down there. You can't let people come and go as they please."

Reflective way of giving information: Observations (facts) and inferences: "Twice this week at starting time, I've heard conversations in the corridor that leads into your department. On both occasions I've seen at least three people arriving at work between fifteen and twenty-five minutes late. I'm troubled because the two of us have already talked about the negative effects of lateness on employees and managers of other departments, and I see no improvement."

In these examples, the reflective way of giving information is more effective, since it gives the listener a specific, concrete, quantifiable picture of what the speaker saw happen and its impact on the speaker. This heightens the possibility that the listener can choose to respond by taking the speaker into account, rather than simply reacting defensively to an accusation.

Yes, But: Giving Observational Data

- "But won't people dismiss my data as inconsequential?" One perceived threat of presenting observational data is that it (and we) will be dismissed as having no grounds for concern or overreacting. It doesn't make sense to present what we predict will make us vulnerable to abuse.

- "This 'When, I Feel, Because' thing is just coming down too hard on people." Giving data in the "When, I Feel, Because" format increases harshness and blame in interactions, when the purpose is to decrease harshness and blame. Why be unnecessarily harsh and blameful? Behaving in this way makes no sense.

- "Using I-statements feels as if I'm talking to adults as if they were children." The emphasis on giving observable data — specific, concrete, and quantitative — appears to many of us as a request to talk down to people. It would predictably increase defensiveness, not promote inquiry. If the stated intent is to advance interpersonal learning, then how can giving data and triggering defensiveness in the other party help?

- "I'd be robbing the other person of presenting his or her point of view." We are often reluctant to go first and give someone negative information because that would inhibit the other person's expression. We want to invite, not inhibit hearing, the other person's point of view. So it makes no sense to disclose first.

- "Analyzing information ahead of time makes the whole interaction too contrived." We do not want to plan everything out and drain the interaction of spontaneity. We know that some analysis and organization of data about someone's performance is necessary before presenting it. But isn't all this scripting about specifics going too far?

This book invites readers to work through these initial conundrums by joining the lead characters in the stories in Chapter Four as they attempt to enact the ideas about reflective behavior presented in the first four chapters of the book. Below, some of the advantages of giving good data are discussed.

Why Give Observational Data? The interpersonal world tends to operate on inference-level information. We don't usually give the observational-level data that led to our inferences. When we speak about our inferences reflexively, they are mostly judgmental or accusatory in nature. So we put the other person in a position of vulnerability. Unless the person has the presence of mind to ask, "What have you seen that's led you to that negative conclusion?" the person reacts reflexively. He or she feels blamed and may blame in return.

By contrast, if we give the other person access to what we saw as well as what we made of it (our inference), we are risking vulnerability. We are revealing the relationship between our observations and inferences, thereby allowing the other person to question our data as well as the relationship between our data and inferences. The other person might point out that the relationship between the two is questionable or might offer his or her own data that could bring ours into question.

By risking vulnerability rather than creating it in the other person, we help create conditions for reciprocal inquiry. As a result of our initiative, the other person may choose to reveal observations and inferences rather than assert inferences as if they were correct simply because they were thought and spoken. With both of us disclosing our observational data and related thinking, each of us has the opportunity to find out something new:

- Maybe our observational data are limited or faulty.

- Maybe our observational data are correct but the inference we drew from it is incorrect.

- Maybe if the two of us combine our observational data, we will develop more useful inferences than either of us has come up with on our own.

- Maybe we'll see that there is a fundamental difference between the two of us in what we see and make of it. Yet realizing that neither one of us is right or wrong, we can choose to move ahead by flipping a coin or using organizational authority to decide.

Asserting Our Search for Sense

A second kind of giving good information is breaking the habit of giving other people only the product of private sense making and instead speaking that sense-making process out loud, particularly when we are at sea or lost. This allows other people to have access to what is going on inside our minds so they can collaborate with us in searching for new sense.

One way to illustrate the idea of asserting our search for new sense is to show its opposite: hiding our search for sense. Reflexively, we hide our search for sense. Following is a brief excerpt of the beginning of a meeting between a vice president, general manager, and manager. The vice president gives an assignment that neither the general manager nor the manager understands; although they must complete the assignment, both hide their confusion rather than assert it:

1. *Vice president:* We haven't had much time to talk about the approach, but I'm really not so concerned about that because the problem here is really straightforward.

   General manager's internal monologue: "Not much time" is an understatement! I don't want to appear stupid, but I need more clarification. I'm not at all sure of the approach you expect.

2. *General manager:* I think I understand your perspective, but can we talk about the approach a little bit more?

3. *Vice president:* I'm afraid I'm overdue for a meeting, but think about the approach, and if you get stuck, give me a call. I've got full confidence in the team, and given that the problem is straightforward, you should really have no problem. We should reconvene in two weeks. I'll expect progress updates in the meantime. (The vice president leaves the room.)

   General manager's internal monologue: This looks about as clear as mud. But I can't let the manager think that I'm not on top of things. He'll lose confidence.

4. *General manager:* It's too bad we didn't have more time with the vice president, but I think we've got enough to go on. Let's flesh out the work plan.

Manager's internal monologue: Boy, I'm glad I'm not the one who has to make sense of this. Looks like the general manager is clear on it. It'll probably work out all right.

5. *Manager:* I'm ready. Let's do it.

Were the general manager to have asserted his search for sense when the vice president first spoke, he might have said at statement 2 above, "Actually the problem is not straightforward to me, and I'm not at all sure of the approach you expect. I need to tell you what I'm confused about so you can help me clarify the approach."

Were the manager to have asserted his search for sense to the general manager at statement 5 above, he might have said, "I'm glad you're the one who has to make sense of this because I'm in the dark about what the problem is and the approach expected by the vice president."

Had each man asserted his search for sense as illustrated, he would have created an opportunity for interpersonal learning, with the possible result of clarifying the task before beginning work, thereby decreasing the risk of wasting time, money, and energy by doing the wrong thing.

Out of context, here are additional examples of asserting the condition of searching for sense or no sense:

- "I'm confused. Let me tell you what pieces I've got bouncing around in my brain; then maybe you can help me."

- "I came in here thinking *x*; now you're strongly urging me to do *y*. Let me go back through your reasoning, and you give me feedback. Then I want to play out my reasoning before I decide."

- "You've told me you are overworked and understaffed. I hear the urgency as you speak, and I want to respond to it. I don't want people here to be pushed beyond the brink. It's not good for us personally or as a business. Still, I'm skeptical and puzzled. I want to tell you why and ask you to help me by describing what you are going through. If I can see it, I can understand. Then together, we can figure out whether something can be done to improve things."

The natural discomfort we all feel about asserting ourselves in these ways is illustrated in the case of a manager who makes the final decision about how to respond to emergencies at a nuclear power plant (see the Introduction). He hears the emergency alarm sound, sends an operator to check the control panel at the point of alarm, and listens while the operator reports back a finding that is the exact opposite of what the manager expected.

He is stunned. His sense is fractured. Instantly and totally unexpectedly, he is in no sense. He says to himself, "Oh, no!"

If the manager does what comes naturally, he will not reveal his sense making because he expects himself to have sense made. Ashamed of his failure to comprehend, he hides his confusion. Scrambling privately, he publicly asks questions to satisfy his private, frenetic search for an answer. The worst-case result of this isolation is a failure to use his team members as resources for learning that might improve his decision making.

In contrast, were the plant manager a confident interpersonal learner, he would assert his scramble for new sense so others might join him. Such an assertion might look like this: "Listen up! We've got two minutes until I've got to make a decision. You'll have that decision. Between then and now, I'm going to think out loud, and you're going to interrupt me with new information, including explanations for what's going on. I'm confused by . . . "

He would continue, articulating the discrepancy between the information he predicted getting and what he actually got, how the different result threw his theory into question. He would ask explicitly for input. Staying firmly in charge, he would lead his group in assembling new information, inventing alternative explanations for events, and deciding to act on a diagnosis or procedural sequence he may not have thought of on his own.

Yes, But: Asserting Our Search for Sense

- "Look, I'd just be asking to be taken advantage of." In the interpersonal world, the idea is win or be right. The idea is to be invulnerable. By definition, asserting our search for sense is an effort not to be right or win but to learn, that is, to invite new data, reasoning, or exploration of assumptions hidden in our thinking. In short, asserting our search for sense makes us vulnerable.

- "If you're right that people know only how to view one another as problems, then that's what will happen to me. The other person will just try to fix me!" With the best of intentions, most people offer help in the form of corrective behavior, either as critique or reassurance. Few people have a repertoire of interpersonal learning skills. So the chances of having others join in a two-way process of learning are very slim. Common sense would say not to risk it.

Why Assert Our Search for Sense? When others have access to our search for sense, they can help us improve the quality of our sense making by listening and giving feedback about the process itself: questioning tacit assumptions, causal relationships, or the nature and validity of our data. By going public with the process, we gain the opportunity to learn about it and improve it, where, in contrast, our natural reflexive tendency is to hide it, with the result that we keep making the same mistakes in thinking.

By asserting our search for sense or no sense, we create the conditions within which others might risk doing the same. They can gain confidence in their ability to assert their search for sense rather than hide it and improve the quality of their sense making through interaction with us.

Finally, there are few more potent ways to build trust in relationships than asserting our search for sense. When we do, others feel increased trust in our openness to influence and our willingness and ability to correct mistakes in our thinking and behavior, and they believe what we say about wanting to work with them as partners or as a team. Others feel truly useful, engaged, and connected to us.

Asserting Reflective Assumptions, Perspectives, and Values

Finally, the phrase "giving good information" means not only presenting observational data with inferences and asserting our search for sense; it means asserting the assumptions, perspectives, and values of communication as interpersonal learning, or reflective practice. Illustrations of different contexts in which we must assert the assumptions, perspectives, and values of communication as interpersonal learning follow.

Setting Organizational Expectations for Reflective Behavior

A new school principal meets for the first time with an assistant principal about racial discrimination in the school: "I'll give you a promise to use all of the resources of my position and person to end discrimination in this school. I won't tolerate a blame game. I expect that all of us will examine our behavior and its consequences and causes. None of us is totally at fault for the conditions here, and all of us are partly the cause."

Learning, in the sense of examining and changing one's own thinking and behavior, is explicitly stated as a value and contrasted with the blame-game norm it is meant to replace.

Setting Reflective Guidelines for Participation in Meetings

A new executive presented the following list of reflective guidelines at the first meeting with her executive team. Then she engaged the group in discussion about what it would take to act on the guidelines. As the discussion proceeded she made public lists of obstacles, costs, and pay-offs.

1. Claim personal responsibility rather than blame.

2. Reveal uncertainty as well as conclusions.

3. Search for new sense as well as make points.

4. Welcome no sense, and articulate it instead of bluffing.

5. Assert inquiry as well as argument.

6. Seek empathic understanding rather than problem-solve people.

7. Pursue feedback rather than defend.

8. Use feedback to gain insight.

9. Translate insight into new behavior.

10. Ask for help.

Explaining Our Own Reflective Behavior in a One-to-One Exchange

A manager repeatedly left his office to solve a particular kind of computer problem for an employee who, the manager believed, should have been solving the problems on his own. The manager punctuated each rescue with a reflexive admonition, "You've got to learn to solve these problems on your own!" But the employee continued to come for help. Beside himself, the manager chose to examine his own part in producing this common, debilitating pattern. After a period of personal reflection about his own supervisory practice, he said to the employee: "While it's obviously important for all of us to do our jobs, it's equally important that we learn to examine how we do our jobs, with an eye to improving our performance. I have not been acting on this value myself when I jump up to solve your computer problems. Instead, I should have been figuring out what information and skills allowed me to solve the problem and then teaching them to you. There are analytical tools you need to diagnose and solve these problems yourself. I'm going to help you learn those tools so you'll be able to do on your own what I've been doing for you."

Here, the manager is at once enacting and explaining the reflective value of taking responsibility for his own learning by turning away from blame and toward an examination of his own supervisory practice. He expects the same from his employee and says so, promising a partnership in the learning process.

Yes, But: Asserting Reflective Assumptions, Perspectives, and Values

- "It's a 'bring me solutions, not problems!' world out there! And you think I'm going to assert principles of interpersonal learning! Please." We can predict that the principles, assumptions, and values of the reflexive world will result in people hearing the language of communication as interpersonal learning as a mouth full of mush or ivory tower hogwash. So it makes no sense to assert reflective assumptions, perspectives, and values.

- "People have been shot for advocating heresy in public." Asserting reflective assumptions, perspectives, and values is heresy. It violates the norm of speaking to show that you know and can do. Predictably, we could be attacked or insidiously dismissed in any number of pejorative ways: as not having what it takes, as dragging down the group, as being stupid, incompetent, or weak, for example. It makes no sense to assert the values of communication as interpersonal learning.

Why Assert Reflective Assumptions, Perspectives, and Values? Reflective practice is a commitment to changing the nature of communication from protective and corrective to interpersonal learning. To make a case for change, we must be able to describe the patterns of behavior that characterize each mode, as well as the antecedents and consequences of these different patterns. This requires that we understand, articulate, and assert reflective assumptions, perspectives, and values.

Apart from advocacy, our effectiveness in communicating to learn depends on our ability to articulate reflective assumptions, perspectives, and values—and at the right time. The right time is often before we behave reflectively; it is then that we need to articulate the change we plan to make and why. To explain why we plan to behave differently, we must assert reflective assumptions, perspectives, and values. If we do not, we can predict that the person on the receiving end of our new behavior will attribute conscious negative intent and respond defensively. That is how someone from the reflexive, interpersonal world makes sense of and responds to unexpected behavior.

The Listening Skill, or Getting Good Information: Concepts, Examples, and Rationale

Listening is a behavior. Our behavior follows from our sense making. Our sense making is made up of our thinking and feeling, along with embedded assumptions. As a unit, our behavior, thinking and feeling, and assumptions are our frame of reference. The listening chart shown here in Table 3.1 on the next page juxtaposes two frames of reference that we can use to make sense of the information we receive from another person. It explains why our natural, reflexive form of listening behavior is so different from listening reflectively.

Table 3.1 The Listening Chart Two Frames of Reference	
Reflexive: **People Are Problems**	**Reflective:** **People Are Sense Makers**
1. What's the problem? 2. What's wrong with her/him/them/the situation? 3. What am I going to do to fix it?	1. What do I hear in the tone and what do the words tell me about the source of the tone? 2. Do I hear an implicit hope, intent, fear, plea, need, or assumption? 3. Do I hear reasons or reasoning being presented to explain something? Or, do I hear the sound of someone who is confused and searching, puzzling, trying to put the pieces together? Or, might this person be stuck, at wits end?

The left side of the table, labeled "Reflexive," presents the assumption we make automatically, that people are problems and depicts the questions we ask ourselves when someone speaks to us:

- What's the problem?

- What's wrong with him, or her, or them, or the situation?

- What am I going to do to fix it?

We ask these questions with the intent of making the right interpretation and acting on it. Of course, the questions we ask shape what we hear, and what we hear shapes our listening behavior. Because we ask problem-solving questions, it follows that our behavior will be fix-it or corrective in nature.

In contrast, the right side of the table, labeled "Reflective," presents the assumption we can choose to make: that people are sense makers.[6] It depicts a very different set of questions we can ask ourselves when someone speaks to us. Generically, we ask ourselves, What sense might this person be trying to communicate? We help ourselves answer this question by asking more specific questions to see which one helps us understand. Because we make sense through our feelings as well as our thoughts, we must pay attention to both when we ask ourselves:

- What do I hear in the feeling tone, and what do the words tell me about the source of the tone?

- Do I hear an implicit hope, intent, fear, plea, need, or assumption?

- Do I hear reasons or reasoning being presented to explain something? Or do I hear the sound of someone who is confused and searching, puzzling, trying to put the pieces together? Or might this person be stuck, with no idea of what to do?

We ask these very different questions with the intent of understanding where the other person might be coming from and test our understanding, explicitly, giving the other person an opportunity to say, "Yes, that's it," or, "No, you didn't hear what I was saying," or, "That's part of it, but what I was really trying to say was . . . " In short, our effort is to understand and validate what the other person is trying to communicate in that moment, not to interpret and fix.

To illustrate the difference between reflexive and reflective thinking and consequent listening behavior, four situations follow. In each, someone gives information we dislike, disagree with, or see as wrong. Each situation is followed by an example of typical reflexive thinking and consequent behavior that is then contrasted with an example of reflective thinking and behavior.

Listening, Example One

Context: I've instituted a set of new procedures in the office, and I'm reviewing them with a key employee who says, "I don't know. This is a lot of new stuff all at once, and it's complicated. I'll do my best, but . . . "

Typical reflexive/fix-it response: I might think, "Cut the complaining," or, "You've handled tougher stuff than this." Either thought follows from the question "What's his problem?" Either thought leads inevitably to presenting a solution: one critical, the other reassuring. I might say, "Complaining's not going to get us anywhere. Try it. If you have problems, I'm here," or, "I know you can do it. You've handled more difficult assignments."

Inquiry/listening response: I might think, "What's he feeling, and what gives rise to it?" I could hear the person's apparent uncertainty, resulting from the number and complexity of procedural changes. I might ask, "You're willing to try, but you're uncertain about succeeding because of the amount and complexity of the changes?"

Listening, Example Two

Context: I tell a new employee that I was disturbed with his joking and interrupting in the last staff meeting I ran. The employee says hesitantly, "This is awkward for me to say, but before I joined your group, I heard your meetings were deadly dull. I was trying to make a heavy meeting more bearable."

Typical reflexive/fix-it response: I might think, "You're not going to deflect this onto me!" Here, the reflexive question used to make sense is, "What's wrong with him? What's he up to?" So I say, "You're not listening to me. I don't want you fooling around in meetings!"

Inquiry/listening response: I might think, "Is he trying to tell me something about his intent or hope, as he experienced it?" I'm able to hear that he apparently sees himself as trying to improve the meeting And I ask, "You were trying to help me?"

Listening, Example Three

Context: I tell a colleague that I'm upset with her implication that I was negligent by not getting a memo to her on time when, in fact, she did not tell me when she wanted it. She says, "Look, it was just irresponsible of you not to get me that memo!"

Typical reflexive/fix-it response: I might think, "You've got to be kidding. What's wrong with you?" Clearly, the reflexive question I'm using to make sense is, "What's wrong with her?" And I say, " You're the one who didn't set a deadline!"

Inquiry/listening response: I might think, "What's in the feeling tone that might tell me what she is trying to convey?" so I would be able to hear her apparent disappointment, as related to my not meeting the deadline. And I ask, "I let you down?"

Listening: Example Four

Context: I call a supervisor whom I manage into my office to talk about her performance in dealing with one of her people. She says in a somewhat desperate tone, "What am I going to do with this guy? He never gets to work on time! I've tried everything and nothing works!"

Typical reflexive/fix-it response: I might think, "So what's her problem?" Here, I am using the question, "What's her problem?" in order to make sense, so I have no choice but to give a solution. I might say, "Look, get rid of him if he can't get his act together."

Inquiry/listening response: I might think, "Where is this woman in her sense making?" so I can hear that she is apparently stuck, at the end of her rope. I might say, "You're at your wits' end?"

Generally, in contrast to the reflexive responses, reflective responses:

- Inquire for understanding rather than give information to convince, improve, change, or solve

- Stay close to the information (in words, tone, and demeanor) given by the other person rather than make leaping inferences

- Come to a full stop and wait for confirmation or disconfirmation

Yes, But: The Listening Skill

Juxtaposed to typical reflexive responses, the reflective responses above can appear at best novel and at worst nonsensical, perhaps even ridiculous. They prompt a general set of predictable, incredulous responses to reflective listening:

- "It's obvious, what he said!" As we begin to listen reflectively, the effort seems absurd because it often appears that what the other person said is already obvious. Reflective listening seems to call for repeating the obvious. This makes no sense at all, since doing so would provoke defensiveness, not encourage inquiry.

- "I tried it and nothing came to mind! Where do you come up with that stuff?" When we throttle our urge to give information and attempt to pay attention to the other person's sense making, we fear that nothing will come to mind, we'll draw a blank, or we'll experience paralysis of analysis. Unfortunately, these fears are often realized during our initial attempts to listen reflectively. As a result, we wonder if it makes sense to risk the pain that accompanies a learning process of such uncertain outcome.

- "What next? Where is this supposed to go?" Most of us puzzle about what is supposed to happen if we are able to invent and use a listening response. We imagine the other person saying back, "Yes, that's right. Exactly!" only to see ourselves staring in silence, our mouths full of marbles, wishing we hadn't made such fools of ourselves.

- "She's just going to take control of the interaction!" Predictably, we fear loss of control. We worry that if we listen, we will not be able to get our point across, which is the purpose we have in most interactions. Should we listen, we reason, the other person will run off with the interaction, taking it off on tangents and into topics we did not come to talk about. So listening goes against our purpose for the interaction. That makes no sense.

- "If I listen, that will make it true! I don't want any part of that." Some of us anticipate that if we listen, we may actually hurt the person we are trying to help. For example, if we sense that a person is trying to communicate disappointment to us, some of us may balk at actually saying, "You're disappointed?" because that would be tantamount to welcoming into existence the very negative feeling that we would want to rescue the speaker from experiencing. So listening would make no sense.

- "No way! In real life, there isn't time to do all this!" Many of us worry that if we throttle the urge to give information immediately and try to listen, our interactions will take longer. We are already too busy, so it would make no sense to add to our already overextended lives.

Choosing to invent and use a reflective listening response, particularly when we are new at it, can feel tantamount to jumping off a cliff with no sense of what purpose it will serve. We anticipate a sorry arrival at the bottom because the answer to our obvious question, "Where might this get me?" is, "On the chasm floor!" This fear can prevent us from listening even when we know that acting reflexively does not work.

Fortunately, practice eases our fears. They are eased even more if someone actually listens to us. Having received the gift, we can imagine offering it and achieving a positive consequence that outweighs the immediate pain of practicing behavior that seems ridiculous.

Listen When You Are Hurting. You need to listen the most when you feel like listening the least: when you are in pain. On the receiving end of information that you do not want to hear, the feelings you have will be a form of pain. Pain can be slight, like a feeling of concern or irritation, or mild, like frustration or being upset, or strong, like outrage or hopelessness.

Reflexively, you will make sense of your pain in one of only two ways: "I have been wronged and need to set this right" or "I did wrong and need to set this right." Your urge will be to rid yourself of the pain, and you will feel compelled to do so by taking corrective action toward others or yourself. Before you act on this reflexive relationship to your pain:

- You must choose to access the reflective perspective that your first priority is learning, not ridding yourself of pain by correcting others or protecting yourself against being hurt. You say to yourself, "This is only pain [as opposed to a sign that I have been wronged or committed a wrong]. I can comfort myself in pain while I act to learn."[7]

- Listening is how you act to learn, and your listening is informed by the reflective idea that people are sense makers, so the sense that the sender of the message conveys might be different from the sense that you receive.

Rather than react by speaking your sense back to the sender, you need to process the message a second time through a set of reflective questions that might help you hear where the sender is coming from:

- What's the central feeling? What's in the content that seems to cause it?

- What's the implicit hope, intent, or fear?

- Is sense made and being handed over? Lost and being looked for? Or, is the person stuck?

Why Use the Listening Skill?

As an idea, listening makes sense. People should listen to one another. In practice, though, it often seems nonsensical, as evidenced in the "yes, but" examples previously. To bridge the gulf between listening as an idea and listening as an integral part of our behavioral repertoire, we must remind ourselves of why we need to listen:

1. *To connect with people.* People are sense makers. If we don't listen to sense making, we're not listening to people.

2. *To produce trust.* Trust is the bedrock of relationships that are enriching and productive. Listening can foster trust, just as not listening can foster mistrust.

3. *To produce valid data.* Reflective listening lets the listener learn if the inference he or she drew from what the speaker said is accurate for the speaker. If the speaker says, "Yes, that's it," the listener can proceed, confident in having a shared base of data. If disconfirmed, the listener can inquire further to reach understanding. In addition, reflective listening lets the speaker decide if he or she actually meant what he or she said. The listener provides the speaker with a moment of reflection-then-commitment. The speaker says,

   - "Yes, that's what I mean. I trust that you know what I know at this moment," or

   - "No. I do not trust that you know where I am coming from," or

   - "Not quite. What I meant was . . . Let me make a statement closer to what is on the mark."

   Thus, the speaker is given an opportunity to embrace, reject, or reform. He or she gets to reflect on and decide whether to place trust in the information as valid.

4. *To break the competition for listening.* Listening to a person as a sense maker rather than as a problem is the only way to break the competition-for-listening pattern of normal conversation. Normally, someone gives us information, thereby tacitly asking us to listen. We give information back, thereby tacitly saying, "No, I cannot listen to you; you listen to me." We

can break this pattern of shoving information back and forth by responding directly to the tacit request for listening.

5.   *To enable learning.* Once we feel heard, we are more open to questioning, discovering, and taking responsibility for the assumptions embedded in our sense making.

Commentary: Which Changes First—Behavior or Sense Making?

The journey from communication as fixing people to communication as interpersonal learning progresses from change in sense making to change in behavior. First come the phases of discovery and invention, then practice and action. This progression is logical but not necessarily accurate.

"Yours is not to reason why, but to do and . . . " is the sentiment of a coach, teacher, drill sergeant, weight-loss facilitator, or boss who expects change in behavior first. It does not matter whether the directive makes sense. The imperative is to do it and trust that new sense will follow. Sometimes it does. But sometimes it does not. When it does not, the new behavior often remains a new hat on the same old head, a superficial technique or method. Because no new sense emerges to back up the new behavior, it is empty, a hollow form. Millions of us change behavior every year in weight-loss programs, only to gain it back because the way we make sense of who we are did not change sufficiently to sustain the new behavior.

At the other extreme, imagine a counseling interaction where thinking is shared for the purpose of gaining insight into embedded assumptions. When discovered, the assumptions are questioned and changed so new behavior can emerge. Sometimes it does. Then again, sometimes it doesn't. People can change the sense they make and yet behave the same. New self-knowledge does not guarantee new behavior. "The insights I had into why I talk too much were stunning," reports a colleague who attended a professional growth seminar, only to continue talking for an hour in praise of the experience.

Obviously, the process of change can begin with new behavior or new sense. It is often impossible to tell where the process began, but it is clear that the value of the journey is eventually to be found in moving out of the protected setting of practice and into real-world action.

Chapter Four

Action: Walking the Talk

It takes courage enough to discover your own reflexive voice, invent a new reflective voice, and practice new behavior in a protected setting. It takes continuing courage to behave reflectively in the real word. Your courage needs to be tempered with the ability to evaluate and choose the right situations for the reflective approach and to apply the reflective skills in the appropriate ways to match those contexts. Such discrimination is necessary because your new behavior will likely catch people off guard, triggering their reflexive sense making—"What's he or she up to?"—followed by a reflexive reaction. Particularly during your first efforts in the real world, you will find such reflexive reactions challenging because you will wish for the other person to applaud your new behavior, not question it, and you will find it difficult not to turn reflexive yourself.

This part of the book offers guidance and examples of taking action at different levels of skill, in a variety of situations presenting different degrees of challenge. Additional guidance is provided in the practice and action sections of Chapter Five.

Assessing the Context and Sequencing the Skills

Contexts for Taking Action at the Outset

Start with a child of your own, if you have children. You can make mistakes with relatively little consequence, and they will make mistakes. As well, children reveal their emotions, so you can see and hear how reflective responses have a different impact. You need to see and hear to believe that reflective behavior makes a difference, and you need to believe to build confidence in your reflective voice. (Other contexts for taking action with each of the individual skills are provided in the "how-to" sections of Chapter Five.)

If you do not have children, start with trusted adults in your home and work life. Begin with a relationship where you can talk with the other person about your desire to communicate differently, and with that person, clarify how and why you want to do this. Then see if the person is willing to join. In this instance, structuring is a kind of contracting. (Of course, you would not do this unless the person and relationship is important to you.)

At work, you can look for opportunities to use your skills quite apart from taking the initiative to structure a change in how you communicate with a trusted person who is important to you. Look for situations where a person is clearly seeking your help in thinking something through, for example:

- Supervision. Often people come to leaders looking for a sounding board or saying they want advice but looking for a sounding board.

- Boss to trusted assistant or confidant

- Close partnerships in sharing leadership

Similarly, you might begin using your skills in a small group where there is a compelling need to continuously put heads together to figure out what is going on and how to respond; everybody knows that there are no answers, only a need to figure out answers. Or the small group could have attended a seminar together that established a shared language for changing communication from fix-it to sense making.

Finally, you might begin using your skills in a crucial situation where you have exhausted your communication-to-fix repertoire without success and you know it, yet you need to produce learning, change, and growth.

Surely this may seem a minimalist approach to taking action successfully, particularly given the nasty situations most of us need to find better ways to handle. Though minimalist, these contexts will most predictably match the level of skill available to us when we first take action. As we gain confidence, our perception of what is possible changes, and we see and make opportunities to apply new skills.

As well, the number of contexts that welcome a reflective approach to communication is increasing. More and more, we are thrown from having sense made into searching for sense by the conditions that define modern life: rapidity of change, complexity, interdependence, and diversity. These conditions constantly disturb the sense we have made and throw us into sense-making soup. As a result, reflective skills are becoming more and more essential to a world that will depend on our ability to lead and learn from each other.[1]

Where People Actually Take Action: Difficult Cases

Although people know that they should begin in the rational, measured way just presented, they tend not to. In fact, most people take action with difficult cases, at home or work. Desperation is the usual cause: "I don't need help with people I trust. I need help with the jerks, and I need it now!"

So instead of providing illustrations of taking action that correspond with the recommended contexts where you should begin, a set of more typical difficult cases is provided here. These difficult cases take one of two forms that exist in everyday life: we must respond to an interaction initiated by someone else, or we initiate the interaction. (Other contexts for taking action with each of the individual skills of structuring, giving good data, and listening are provided in the "how-to" sections of Chapter Five.)

When we respond to interaction initiated by others, as do the lead characters in the first group of stories in this chapter, the challenge to our skill level is that we are taken by surprise: we unexpectedly experience a sense of immediate threat of attack (or of being ignored) by another person. Most often, these are single-incident interactions, in contrast to an interaction where a pattern of past performance is the topic for the meeting.

When we initiate an interaction that we would call difficult, as in the second group of stories here, we are likely to be addressing a pattern of behavior, not a single incident. The challenge is heightened because of having failed in prior fix-it attempts with the person involved. Such situations are difficult because patterns of behavior are very hard to change, even if a person recognizes the patterns as negative and wants to change.

There is little chance of success in these cases unless we practice rigorously, including the collection and analysis of the pattern data, invention and rehearsal of an opening statement that structures the interaction, and ready ability to listen to the predictably different data and views expressed by the other person.

Difficult Cases Are About Exchanging Negative Performance Data

Whether the interactions are initiated by the other person and single incident in nature or initiated by us and focused on patterns of behavior, difficult cases always involve the need to exchange feedback about negative performance, by far the most difficult situations to talk about.

On the job, most people are comfortable talking about the content of their work. They have sense already made of their work content, so they feel confident discussing it. But bring up process issues (how people get the work done) and they feel less comfortable, and they are decidedly uncomfortable with relationship or personal performance issues.

Relationship or personal performance issues raise strong emotions in both parties, making it extremely difficult to think (a precondition of reflective practice) rather than simply react (reflexive practice). The exchange of negative information also rattles the sense we have made, causing confusion and a search for new sense because the other person almost always disagrees, presents negative data about our performance, and balks at our requests or demands.

At the very least, the moral here is to be aware that when you take on a difficult situation, it is difficult for the very reason that you will be trying to talk about what no one wants to talk about, and not without good reason. In fact, most of our experience in dealing with negative performance information is negative, at home and work.

Sequencing the Skills and Assessing Risk

When negative feedback is involved, taking action flounders for lack of fluid control of the three skills that results only from sufficient practice. Operationally, it tends to feel like this: "What in the world do I do next?!" We are talking here about the ability to sequence the skills when under the pressure of a face-to-face exchange that involves negative feedback about both persons' performance. (A model for beginning as receiver and as initiator is provided in the Practice section of Chapter Five.)

The five stories that follow present a progression in level of challenge relative to sequencing the skills, ranging from a single listening response, to a combination of two skills, to a complex sequence of all three skills:

Story	Level of Difficulty
"Million Dollar Listening"	One skill: a single listening response
"You're Never on Time!"	Two skills: a sequence of listening responses and a single "When, I Feel, Because" giving of good data
"I'll Go to the IFO."	Sequence of two of the three skills: listening and structuring
"They Come Back with the Same Problems!"	Sequences of all three skills
"Who Said I Go Overboard?"	Sequences of all three skills

The stories also illustrate different degrees of risk posed by the situation in which the lead character must perform. To this point, our discussion of assessing risk has focused primarily on whether the performance data being exchanged are about a single incident or a pattern of behavior. There is a broader set of criteria, displayed in Table 4.1 on the next page.

Table 4.1 Criteria for Assessing Degree of Risk in Difficult Interactions		
Criterion[a]	**Lower Risk**	**Higher Risk**
Other person	Interpersonal sense maker	Fault-finding fixer
Nature of the data	Content data or technical data	Process, or relationship and performance data
Incident or pattern	Single incident	Pattern
Relationship	High trust	Low trust
Stake in the outcome	Equal	Unequal
Positional relationship	Subordinate, colleague, family member	Boss, client
Shared culture/ "language"	Yes	No
Continuity of contact	Over time	One-shot deal
Commitment of lead person	High (will commit extra time)	Low (will give only one meeting)

[a]Sequencing the skills successfully under the pressure of exchanging negative performance data is so difficult that unless you practice, there is little hope of not reverting to fix-it communication and getting stuck in a competition-for-listening exchange. In part, this is true because of this principle: you cannot give negative performance feedback without getting it in return.

The stories in this chapter present a range of contexts, each meeting some lower-risk and some higher-risk criteria, but generally increasing from lower to higher risk, culminating in a story of a challenging and risky interaction.

When taking action in these dialogue stories, the lead characters will be:

- Groping to discover when their minds are controlled by their own reflexive, fix-it frame of reference

- Choosing to risk breaking reflexive habits of thought and action and invent reflective possibilities

- Attempting to use a single reflective skill, combination of two skills, or all three skills together in sequences.

The action takes place both at home and in a variety of work settings. The hope tacit in providing different settings is to increase the possibility that readers will find a lead character to identify with and thereby engage in a personal growth process of discovery, invention, and practice through a vicarious participation with the lead characters. The lead characters' internal monologues invite participation in the process of discovering our reflexive frame of reference and inventing a reflective alternative. The interpersonal dialogues provide an opportunity to practice translating reflective ideas into new behavior.

Imaginatively, put yourself in the position of the lead character. Before you read what the lead character says back to a son, mate, client, employee, or boss, write down the best reflective response you can invent. Compare what you wrote to what the lead character says.

The stories are presented in two groupings: responding to a single incident and initiating to address a pattern of behavior.[2]

Responding to a Single Incident

Story: Million Dollar Listening

The lead character here produces one listening response that creates a multimillion-dollar opportunity. In one sense, the story is an example of a beginning level of application of the skills, since there is no sequencing. But that does not mean that what the lead character achieves is easy. To take action successfully, we must have developed confidence in a new, reflective voice that guides the action we take. This story features the character's internal monologue, where he demonstrates his ability to discover his entrapment in reflexive thinking and to extricate himself by calling on a new reflective voice to guide him in taking action.

I am an owner of an architectural firm. One day I received a call from an Italian man who was in the United States to choose an architectural firm for a project that he described vaguely, mentioning the need to simulate a building on computer before it was constructed. I assured him that we had done many computer simulations. When he arrived, I had our computer specialist demonstrate our ability to simulate a building on computer and showed that we had worked extensively with the Ivy League school that has the best computer in the country for this type of simulation. Still, as we talked, the man's words were perfunctory in tone.

For half an hour we showed him our computer capability and the buildings we had designed using it. Yet he continued to speak of the need for simulating the building in advance of building it, as if he were not looking at the computer demonstration or hearing any of my explanations of our proficiency and track record.

After the tour of our office and computer demonstration, I sat with the man to hear him out. He said he was the final decision maker for choosing an architect to build a $50 million research center and, to follow, a $500 million research center. Need I say he had my full attention?

The man talked discursively and abstractly for more than ten minutes, first about a quality of weightlessness being essential to the design of the building: "This must be the feeling inside and viewing from different vantage points outside—a lightness, an elevating spirit."

Then he went on, apparently on a different tack: "During the design process, it will be important to simulate the use of the building, so that we know how the space can be used. This will be very important to me." He continued, "How will it appear to the people who use it? We must see how it will appear to the people who will work in the different spaces. We must have a feel for the space before we build."

He kept going: "I want to see how people will move around in the different parts of the building as different events occur at the same time. Ahead of time, we should understand the building by computer. If a lecture, a seminar, and a demonstration are all occurring at once, how will people will move and not disturb others at work? They must be separate but together in the same space." He paused. Then he continued, "If there's a fire, where will everyone go?"

There, he stopped.

The stop was unexpected and as abrupt a contrast as I could imagine to his meandering presentation.

As I sat silently while the man talked, I was excited by the enormous opportunity he seemed to represent. At the same time, I was skeptical and frustrated with his lengthy, obscure, and repetitive talk. After all, I had already shown him we could produce major buildings with a computer and had a sophisticated computer system and were willing to associate with the university that has the best computer in the country for this type of simulation.

I wondered why he kept repeating the same thing (was he dense or what?) and wished he would stop talking so I could tell him again that we were the right firm for these projects. Yet I was aware that telling him this over and over again was not working.

Then I had a crashing visual insight: while I was looking at his behavior and thinking he was dense, he was probably looking at my behavior and thinking I was dense! As long as I thought he was dense, I had to straighten him out, pitch him to the right way of thinking—that is, to *my* way of thinking. But if he was looking at my behavior, at my repetitive pitches, his sense making could be, "Is this guy [referring to me] ever going to get it? How many times do I have to repeat myself before he gets what I'm trying to say? What's his problem? Is he dense, like the rest of the architects I've spoken to?" I was seeing his inner world, from the inside out, so to speak, and realizing that there wasn't something wrong with him that needed correction by me.

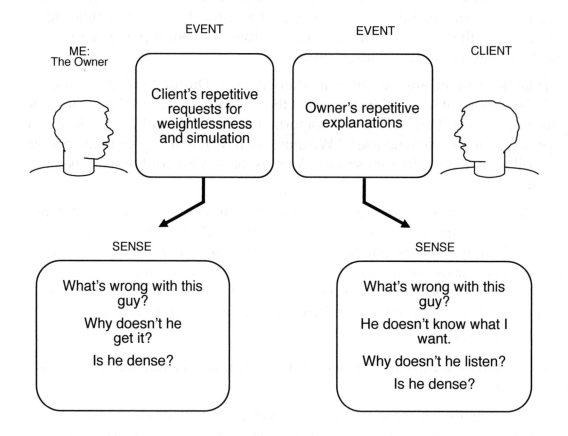

Instead of continuing in my habitual manner of trying to right the wrong of his thinking by repeating my pitch, I forced myself to think differently. In the privacy of my mind, I said: "Try to listen; risk testing if you get it in his terms. Maybe he's repeating himself because he feels you're not getting it." This apparently innocuous request of myself made me feel silly. I was fighting off a different voice in my head saying, "He knows what he said! Get on with it!"

Still, haltingly, I took the plunge, forcing myself not to presume that I was reading the situation right but instead to check it out. I asked, "You're not so sure I know what's important to you, are you?"

"No," he said, imperceptibly.

I continued, "I want to make sure I'm getting this right, so bear with me. You're looking for a building that will embody a quality of weightlessness in both the interior and exterior presentation?"

I stopped because I was unsure of myself, and I wanted confirmation from him that I was on the right track. Maybe I'm wrong but his face seemed to soften a bit. In any case, I went on with my paraphrase after a moment or two. "Throughout the design process, you want a firm that can use a computer to model different ways to use the space, as an aid in your decision making?"

I paused until he nodded. His eyes had joined mine, finally. This made it easier for me to continue. "Through the simulation, you want the people who will work in the building to see what each space might look and feel like, and it is very important for you to see ahead of time the movement patterns in the building. For example, when there are multiple events going on, you want to be sure with your own eyes that the pattern of movement does not interrupt people who are not involved in the events."

Again, I waited until he nodded and said, "Yes, yes," with mild enthusiasm.

I went on, "You want every detail to be thought through thoroughly. The fire exits and procedure are only one example of that?" As I heard myself say these words, I realized that now I was doing more than paraphrasing his words alone. I had just answered the question about what sense he was trying to convey. He seemed to want an exacting attention to detail.

As I waited, he smiled and spoke pleasantly and firmly, "That's right, yes. It is very important that we get the details correct." As he spoke, he gathered himself upright in his chair, still holding my eyes with his. He had finally decided to attend our meeting.

As I was reiterating what he said, I was asking myself silently the sense-making questions that were so new to me. Does the sense he is trying to convey lie in:

- The feeling tone?
- A tacit concern?
- An intent?
- A hope of some kind?
- A fear I'm not hearing?

That's it! Before I had formed the thought in my mind, I knew it was there and coming out of my mouth: "What it all adds up to is trust — or lack of it? You want to see for yourself on the computer screen what we design, not just be asked to trust only our words and drawings?"

My guest sat as if stunned into silence. Incredulous, he replied with hesitation and then excitement: "Yes, that's what I want. Yes, that is it." He sat, apparently savoring the moment, and then finished: "You are the first person in the United States who has listened to me and understood what I want! I am very pleased." He paused, stood, and walked around the room saying that he had seen three national firms the day before and planned to visit one more the next day, adding that unless the next firm could do better, he had already made his choice in favor of my firm.

Commentary

The question often arises: Did he get the job? But in the context of this book, the question should be: Did he create opportunity where before there was none? The answer to this question is a resounding yes. And he did it by taking action to invent new thinking and behavior in the moment, in the context of desperately scrambling to make new sense.[3] In this internal condition, he had the confidence and ability to shift his mind-set and consequently his behavior from reflexive to reflective and risk acting "funny" in the real world.

Surely, the architect exhausted his reflexive repertoire before he risked reflective behavior. That is not unusual. Often we have to be pushed right to the limits of our fix-it (pitch it) repertoire before we take action in a reflective form. Here, the lead character had done enough practice (as evidenced in the richness of his internal dialogue about the difference between reflexive and reflective thinking) to substantially increase the likelihood of success in taking action.

Story: You're Never on Time!

The lead character here produces two skills and a sequence of listening responses rather than a single iteration. She uses the skills of listening and of giving good information after an accusation by her husband. Her internal monologue shows her struggle to make sense reflectively instead of relying on her reflexive judgmental thinking. She conveys the excitement of experiencing for the first time how her listening and feedback skill changes her husband's behavior toward her.

My name is Rita. I was working late and had to pick up my husband from the airport. He told me to check with the airline before coming, so I called and found it was snowing in Chicago. The agent on the phone told me to call back in an hour because the plane would probably be delayed for hours. When I called back, I was told by another agent that the plane had landed at the airport fifteen minutes ago. In my rush, I took a wrong turn, and it took me more than an hour to get there. Len had been waiting for an hour and a half and was livid when he got in the car.

"Hello," I said brightly.

He snarled, "You're never on time! How could you treat me this way?"

I was hurt (even though I am late more often than not). I fought back, "I called the airline and they gave me the wrong information!"

He talked right over me. "How could you be so late? I told you to call the airline! Can't you dial a number?"

I shouted, "Don't you accuse me of not doing what I did!" and went on to tell my story about calling twice and taking the wrong turn.

"That's a likely story!" he snapped and went on to moan about his terrible week of running after clients, taxis, and airplanes. It was a mess. We sat in the car, both of us seething, waiting for the traffic to move in the tunnel from the airport.

After a while, I thought to myself, "Why am I being defensive about this? This is really insane." Although I was hurting inside, I decided to try to jump into his mind and think about what he might have been through during that week away. I realized that he might be very tired, especially after a week of chasing clients and not sleeping in his own bed.

Figuring that I had nothing to lose, I tried to listen, "You're flat out exhausted?"

As if slapped to alertness, he turned to me and said, "I really am. You really hit the nail on the head basically."

Seconds the length of hours passed, and he went on: "I started the day waiting an hour for a client who canceled the appointment and ended the day waiting more than an hour for

you." As he spoke, I told myself, "Don't get defensive. Try to listen. He seems to feel that he's been getting jerked around." So I tested my best idea of what he was asking me to hear: "You've been getting a real runaround?"

"Yes, I have," he said quietly. Making a cutting motion across his forehead, he continued, "I've had it right up to here!"

Bumper-to-bumper with cars in front and behind, we sat in silence. And then he apologized, and he never had before. I was speechless. It seemed that five minutes passed before I got my voice back. When I did, I accepted his apology. The accusations stopped.

The traffic inched forward. After we got out of the tunnel, we had a pleasant conversation for the remainder of the ride home.

Even as we rode along, I knew that our conflict had ended because I decided to stop insisting that he listen to my problems. Instead, I listened to him, even though I was hurt by his accusation. I couldn't believe how it worked to listen. It was new to me. Looking back, I know I was frightened by the power in it.

Still, I fretted all night about his accusation that I did not care enough to treat him right . . . I was about to say to him, "Len, you shouldn't speak to me the way you did last night, accusing me of not caring enough to be on time." But I thought to myself, "Wouldn't he say back, 'You shouldn't keep me waiting for an hour and a half, even if you didn't mean it'?" Then the fight could be on again.

So while he was shaving, I tried to give him good information about where I was coming from by using the "When, I Feel, Because" format to guide me in giving good information. I said, "Len, when you accused me of not caring enough to be on time, I was hurt and could not sleep. My being late had nothing to do with caring. It had to do with bad information and a driving mistake. I was really looking forward to seeing you!" He said, surprised, "Waiting at the airport last night was just the last straw. I was angry at you and afraid for you. I thought maybe you had an accident. I just lost it." We talked for a while and then had a lovely weekend.

Commentary

When we feel attacked and hurt by someone else, we often choose to act toward that person from this pain as if the only way to make sense of the situation were through the attribution to him or her of conscious intent to do us wrong. Rita chose to do exactly this in the moment after Len made the accusation, "You're never on time. How could you treat me this way?"

She was hurt and struck back, explaining herself: "I called the airline and they gave me the wrong information!"

The result here and in similar circumstances in our own lives is a fight and, over time, the loss of intimacy and the opportunity to gain new understanding of one another.

Listening. Rita shows us that there is an alternative to reflexively acting from the pain and the related inference that Len could only be consciously out to get her. Initially, she strikes back at Len, but a few minutes later, she begins to reflect and chooses to use the idea of empathic listening to guide her inquiry into what might be going on here rather than continuing to choose her pain as the source for making sense: "Even though I was hurting inside, I decided to try to jump into his mind and think about what he might have been through during that week away."

She chose to think imaginatively and act empathetically, reaching out to see the world as her husband might be seeing it in the moment ("I bet you're flat out exhausted?"; "You've been getting a real runaround?"), and through this effort, she created the conditions where he could take responsibility for his own thoughts and feelings ("Yes, I have," referring to getting the runaround, "I've had it right up to here!"), with the result that he apologized for his behavior.

To behave empathetically when she felt wrongly accused, Rita had to feel capable of taking care of her own pain in the moment of reaching out to Len's side of the world (his pain of exhaustion, anger, fear). If she could not comfort herself reflectively in that moment, her pain would have remained the only source for her sense making, leaving her with only two options: strike back in accusation (as she did initially) or apologize for causing Len's pain.

Giving Good Information. In the morning, when she found herself still concerned, she decided not to continue comforting herself in the silence of her own mind, but to present information about what she heard Len say ("when you accused me of not caring enough to be on time") separated from the sense to her in feeling ("was hurt ") separated from the impact on her ("could not sleep. My being late had nothing to do with caring. It had to do with bad information and a driving mistake. I was really looking forward to seeing you!"). She shaped her thinking with the "When, I Feel, Because" format for giving good information. In this way, she avoided being judgmental and beginning a new round of accusations.

Story: I'll Go to the IFO. They'll Get You!

Like the prior stories, this is a single-incident, difficult case. But here, for the first time, we see a lead character sequence two of the three skills as follows: listening, structuring, listening, structuring. Midstream in a reflexive confrontation, the lead character discovers himself shooting the rapids of a bitter and potentially costly conflict. He pulls himself from the flow of argument and proposes a reflective restructuring of the dialogue to break the competition-for-listening pattern. Then he uses the listening skill to begin the process of joint problem solving and structures the end of the exchange to guarantee results.

I am the manager of an internal auditing group in a power plant. A new manager of another group outside mine angrily burst through the door of my director's office into a private meeting between my director and me. I had denied a change-in-procedure he requested because the manager he replaced had made the same request, which I approved but the manager did not act on before he left his position. If an approved request is not acted on and the closure reported to the regulatory agency overseeing our operations, we can be sanctioned.

A sanction is no small matter. Our plant, like all other power plants, is under the strict control of a regulatory commission (IFO). If the IFO sanctions the company for some wrongful or illegal practice, it can cost big money, lost reputation in the industry, and public relations nightmares. If there are a given number of findings, the plant can be shut down.

Approval of the new manager's change meant that the first request and consequent inaction would be subject to review by the regulatory agency. The new manager needed to withdraw his prior manager's request before resubmitting his if we were to avoid unnecessary sanction.

1. He said, giving me information: "I read your reason for disapproving my request, and frankly, I don't believe that's a reason at all. If you believe we acted improperly, you should have filled out an IFO report ability form and then approved my request."

2. I said, giving him information: "The problem was reported once. The resolution was not completed."

3. But before I finished, he interrupted. "You shouldn't hold up my change because someone else did something wrong. Just approve it and handle the other problem separately."

4. I said, giving him information: "I couldn't. They were the same issue. If I approve your change, I'd be exposing us to enforcement from the IFO when we've done nothing wrong."

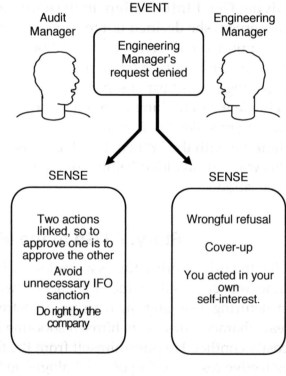

5. He said, giving me information: "So you're covering up a problem the IFO should know about. I'll tell the IFO what you're doing! They'll get you for it!"

At this point, the lead character discovers himself operating within his reflexive frame of reference and realizes he has a choice. He could have continued in a defensive fix-it mode, in which case he would have found himself in the battle illustrated in the left-hand column of the list that follows. Instead, he chose to respond by trying to shift into reflective mode using the structuring and listening skills:

Reflexive Exchange	**Reflective Dialogue**
6. I said, giving information data: "Go ahead! You'll only embarrass yourself and your organization!"	6. I said, attempting to restructure the interaction from reflexive to reflective: "We're not hearing one another, are we? Isn't this just a verbal battle? Let me try stating your position then you listen to mine. Is that okay?"
7. He said, giving me information: "You'll probably lose your job when the facts are known."	7. He said: "Fine."
8. I said, giving him information: "You're telling me I should have blessed it anyway?"	8. I said, attempting to reiterate his point of view: "You think there's no link between the prior manager's request and yours, so I should have served your need for a change immediately. Your need is urgent. You don't trust my assumption about a link, so I seem to have gone out of my way to protect myself somehow and to inconvenience you?"
9. He said, giving me information: "You guys are careful only when it makes someone else's job difficult."	9. He said: "Exactly. That's it."
10. I said, giving him information: "I disapproved it because you did it wrong."	10. I said, attempting to encapsulate my point of view: "Your request and the former manager's request

are linked. If I approve your request, then his inaction will have to be reported to the IFO, even though we have not done anything wrong or illegal. If you do the paperwork to withdraw the original request, and then resubmit yours, I can approve yours; you can take action and report the closure without threat of sanction for the prior inaction."

11. He said, giving me data: "You're the one who did it wrong! This was a high-visibility corporate commitment. You stonewalled my change. When the vice president finds out what you did, you'll be fired!"

11. He said, listening to me: "So you were trying to keep us from getting unnecessarily embarrassed by the IFO?"

12. I said, confirming that I felt heard: "Exactly."

13. He said, giving me information: "I'm now clear on why you did it. But we need the change as soon as possible."

14. I said, trying to structure the next step for resolution and closure: "Before you leave here momentarily, I'll put in your hands the paperwork you need to withdraw the prior request. Get it to me today? Today I'll confer with my investigator, you with your supervisors. You find out from them the date you can begin work with my investigator. Let's talk before 6:00 P.M., when we'll settle on the date and the timing of your resubmitting your new request for a change. When I get it, I'll approve it. Sound okay?"

15. He said, confirming the structure I proposed: "Yes, okay. I'm writing a few notes. I'm glad we discussed this. It prevented a serious misunderstanding."

Commentary: Criteria for Taking Action on a Difficult Case

As with the preceding two stories, the IFO story illustrates a situation in which the lead character must respond to a single incident. Suddenly confronted by a very angry fellow manager, he uses two reflective skills (listening and structuring) to break the competition-for-listening pattern and defuse a potentially explosive conflict.

In the stories that follow, the focus shifts from single incidents to interactions about patterns of behavior. The stakes are higher when addressing a pattern of negative performance, and a more complex sequencing of all three skills is required. When taking action in such cases, it is useful to assess the situation ahead of time using the criteria presented in Table 4.1. Below, you will find more detailed definitions of these criteria, illustrated with examples from the stories. They are provided with the hope that they may help you understand some of the forces at work in difficult case interactions. Difficult case interactions are the focus here because people tend to take action in difficult case circumstances, even though it would make more sense to begin in easy case interactions.

Of course, the lead characters in these first three stories did not assess relative difficulty ahead of time because they did not initiate the interactions. They were caught off guard, thrown into a sense-making situation momentarily, and came out of it deciding to lead with reflective rather than reflexive behavior. In the following two stories where the lead characters take the initiative to address patterns of negative performance, it is self-evident from the skillful structuring and data giving in both stories that the lead characters predicted and anticipated some of the forces they would encounter.

Definitions of Criteria for Taking Action in a Difficult Case

• *Other person's response.* Taking action is lower risk if the other person is willing and able to be reflective and higher risk if not. In the preceding three stories, the potential client, the husband, and the manager are receptive to skillful reflective behavior by one of the lead characters. These lower-risk stories stand in stark contrast to the final story of this section, "Who Said I Go Overboard?" where the other person refuses to engage in interpersonal learning even though the initiator is skillful in sequencing all three skills.

- *Type of data.* Taking action is lower risk if the parties discuss content or technical information and higher risk if they discuss process, relationship, or personal performance information. In "Million Dollar Listening" and "I'll Go to the IFO," the architect and client as well as the two managers are discussing content or technical data. In neither case is the lead character trying to shift the focus of the discussion from content to relationship or performance. In "You're Never on Time," the subject matter is the process of how the wife and husband interact, which makes it a riskier interaction. Both of the following stories involve communicating about performance, which ups the ante considerably.

- *Focus of interaction: Single incident or pattern.* Taking action is lower risk if the parties are focusing on single-incident data and higher risk if they are focusing on a pattern of behavior. In single-incident interactions, such as those in the preceding stories, there is generally less scope and depth of information. In contrast, the following stories deal with patterns of negative performance that have persisted over time. Such patterns tend not to be an accident. They often reflect the nature of a person's sense making and cherished assumptions embedded in it. In effect, when patterns of behavior are questioned, a person's being comes into play. From the outside, we say they get defensive. But from the inside, they feel their integrity is threatened. (For more explanation of the difference between behavior viewed as defensive versus as an expression of integrity, see "Invention: Contrasting Reflexive and Reflective Assumptions about People" in Chapter Five.) Invariably, they respond to the initiator's pattern data by pointing out negative patterns in the initiator's behavior. With negative information about both parties on the table, it is very difficult to conduct an open (reflective) inquiry rather than a closed (reflexive) argument.

- *Relationship: Trust or mistrust.* Taking action is lower risk if there is trust between the parties and higher risk if trust is lacking. By definition, a difficult case involves either a mismatch in level of trust or a shared degree of low (or no) trust. This is true of the stories presented here. A central principle of reflective practice is to interact in a way that maximizes the opportunity to build trust: open, not closed agendas; disclosed, not withheld information; listening for understanding, not acting to fix based on prejudgments. Still, we must be careful not to assume that our intentions are transparent, or that by talking about our intentions, we can talk the other person out of mistrust, or that one reflective interaction will turn mistrust to trust. Prior repeated reflexive behavior contributed to producing the mistrust, and only repeated reflective behavior will gradually produce trust.

- *Stake in outcome: Equal or unequal.* Taking action is lower risk if the parties have an equal stake in the outcome of the interaction and higher risk if they do not. In a difficult case, the stakes are generally unequal at the outset because the person who initiates the interaction wants something from the other person. Initially, at least, the other person has less interest in giving it than the initiator has in getting it. For example, in "Million Dollar Listening" the stakes are clearly unequal between the architect and the prospective client because the client is shopping and can choose other architects. In the stories you are about to read, the mismatch in stake in the outcome is moderate to high risk. In both stories, the lead character asks the other person to reflect on, learn about, and change a pattern the lead character sees as negative, while the other person does not see the pattern or does not see it as negative or want to change it.

• *Position in hierarchy: Equal or unequal power.* Taking action is lower risk if the parties both have the same amount of positional power and higher risk if they hold roles of unequal power. If we talk up the hierarchy, those above us can hurt us more than we them. Talking downward, the imbalance is reversed. The difference in positional power influences what happens in interactions obviously. As committed as we may be to reflective practice, we are probably more committed to our jobs, so we do not want to risk changing the choreography of an interaction with a boss who might see our moves as unusual. It is therefore important to assess the relationship between a boss's pronouncements about communication and his or her actions before taking action. Caution is the word. There are no talking-up-the-hierarchy stories here.

When working down the hierarchy, we must be cognizant of two things: the hierarchical relationship with our subordinates may not matter to us, but we must realize that it matters to them. They are wary about changes we make in the pattern of normal interaction in the same way that we would be wary of changes made by our boss. An unequal hierarchical relationship compounds the way others often receive our well-intentioned efforts to be reflective: if we change our behavior, particularly before first talking about doing it, the other people process that change through their reflexive frame of reference. So for all our good intentions, our reflective behavior will predictably be received at first as indicating that something is wrong and therefore suspect and in need of correction.

• *Shared culture and language.* Taking action is lower risk if the parties share the same cultural norms (and language about how to improve communication) and higher risk if they come from different cultures and do not have a common language of communication. There are no apparent cross-cultural issues in these stories. At the same time, in only one story is risk lowered by the parties' sharing a common language about how to improve communication, along with accompanying expectations for doing so. That appears to happen in the "I'll Go to the IFO" story. Today many organizations sponsor and require attendance at professional growth seminars that establish such a common language, require practicing new skills, and develop a set of expectations for their use.

• *Continuity of contact.* Taking action is lower risk if there is continuity of contact between the parties and higher risk if they are involved in a one-shot deal. The shorter and more sporadic the contact is, the less motivation people have to invest in changing the rules of the game in communicating. It will be self-evident in the following stories that the changes in patterns of behavior sought by the lead characters will not occur without continuity of contact. Changing patterns of behavior, even if we want to change them, is too disruptive, confusing, and difficult to occur without the support of continuous contact.

• *Commitment of person initiating.* Taking action is lower risk if the person initiating the interaction plans to commit extra time to transforming this relationship and higher risk if not. Before taking action on a difficult case, we must assess our degree of commitment to the person whose pattern of behavior bothers us. First, we must look back and assess our degree of exhaustion and exasperation from prior failed attempts. Are we construing this reflective attempt as one last try? If the answer is yes, then the interaction will be high risk because the other person will pick this up and see it as inconsistent with our words pledging commitment. Second, we must look forward and ask ourselves if we are willing to keep this person a priority long enough to get results. Put differently, we must discipline ourselves not to proceed on the false hope that reflective behavior will obviate the need for commitment expressed in action over time.

Initiating to Address a Pattern of Behavior

Story: They Come Back with the Same Problems!

Every time his employees have a problem, this supervisor leaves his office, goes to the employees' desks, and fixes their problems, even though he has repeatedly told them to solve problems for themselves by consulting a manual before they come to him.

Here, he attempts to stop "fixing" and start managing by sequencing the three interpersonal learning skills: structuring, information giving, and listening. First, he structures a meeting with his staff to explain how he intends to change his behavior and why. Then, when an employee asks him to fix something, the supervisor shows in dialogue form how he stops fixing and instead structures the interaction to teach the employee the skills the employee would need to solve the problem.

As a supervisor-coach-teacher, he does not exhibit the normal, reflexive teacher-student or doctor-patient relationship, where one person communicates only to convey information to the other. To the contrary, he demonstrates a reflective partnership in interpersonal learning, where both parties open to examine their own thinking and assumptions, then join in the invention of new thinking and behavior.

I am the cost accountant supervisor in my firm, and I have eight computer operators who report to me. I have been going crazy with each of them coming to me repeatedly with questions that I feel they should be able to answer for themselves. My normal pattern of response is to get up from my desk, go to the person's terminal, figure out what the problem is, and correct it.

The major reason for my frustration has been their lack of response to my insisting that they read the manual before coming to me. In most instances, had they read the manual, they might have figured out the problem on their own. But regardless of how many times I told them to read the manual, they did not do it. Repeatedly they come to me with information, I tell them to read the manual, they give me more information, I tell them to read the manual. It is the competition for listening over and over again!

Three days before the following interaction occurred, I met with all of my computer operators to structure my planned change in behavior by telling them what I planned to do, how I planned to do it, and why I was going to do it. In summary, I said that:

- I was aware that I had told them to come to me when they had problems that could not be solved by consulting the manual.

- In the previous week, each of them had come to me at least twice with problems about which they should have consulted the manual first but did not. I knew they were not consulting the manual because they told me so.

- I was increasingly frustrated because these interruptions were costing me about a half-day a week.

- I intended to try to change my behavior by not jumping up from my desk to solve each problem. Instead, I would teach them the analytical models in my head so they would know when to use the manual and when to come to me.

- I was trying to make this change for two reasons: the cost in my time and personal aggravation was too high, and I had failed to educate them properly. By getting up and going to solve their problems, I was teaching them what a good problem solver I was. So why wouldn't they come to me? In a sense, it was the smart thing to do: come to me and get a right answer fast. Now, though, I planned to teach them how to be better diagnosticians so they could do for themselves what I had been doing. They would advance their skills, and I would eventually free up time I needed for other matters.

A Reflective Dialogue: Structuring to Teach

1. *Employee:* Paul, I have a funny message on my screen.

Structuring

2. *Paul:* Sit down. This will take about twenty minutes. In the past, I'd go to your terminal and figure out the problem for you. As I said in the staff meeting, starting today, I want you to work with me to figure out how to solve the problem on your own.

3. *Employee:* Why don't you just come out? It'll only take a minute.

Listening

4. *Paul:* So this seems a waste of time?

5. *Employee:* Sure. Save time, and do it my way!

Giving Good Data: Observation and Related Inference

6. *Paul:* Okay. I can see why you'd want that. Still, here's my situation: you've been in here five or six times this week, and that's just you. I'm increasingly frustrated because each time I have to stop work and spend five to fifteen minutes addressing the problem you have, I am not doing my own work: planning, supervision, and budget work.

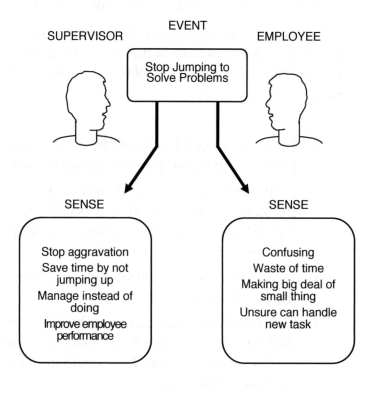

7. *Employee:* But you've said we should come to you with problems.

Listening

8. *Paul:* You're right. And I've said to come after consulting the manual, right? No one is doing that. I'll bet you haven't looked at it today. How come?

9. *Employee:* Okay, okay. We've been through this; you know that manual makes us all spit. People have different reasons, but none of us can make use of the manual. I know you want to change and all, but this will only take a minute! Time is money, Paul.

Structuring

10. *Paul:* You're right. It would save time in the short run and money. But if you can work with me here for a few minutes, it'll pay off in less wasted time and frustration for me, as well as increased skill for you, over the long run.

    Bear with me. Here's what I want you to do: I'll give you a list of events that you will use to identify the kind of error on the screen. There are two types of errors: the funny message is either an application error or a programming error. If it is an application error, consult the manual. If it is a programming error, come back, and you and I will look at it together, or I will work with you at your terminal.

11. *Employee:* Paul, you're making a mountain out of a molehill.

Listening

12. *Paul:* This still isn't making any sense, is it?

13. *Employee:* No, it isn't.

14. *Paul:* I guess you're looking at how we've done business and saying, if it ain't broke, don't fix it?

15. *Employee:* Now we're getting somewhere.

Giving Good Data: Observation and Related Inference

16. *Paul:* It has worked and continues to work for you but not for me because I'm overloaded. So I need you to learn what I know that allows me to fix the funny messages. In the past, I've expected you to consult the manual before coming to me. You haven't. But I still go out. I get annoyed at you and myself because of the cost to my other work. Until recently, I was blind to the fact that I hadn't taught you the information and skill you need to use the manual. It all seemed so straightforward to me.

17. *Employee:* You're not going to let up on this?

18. *Paul:* No. I expect you to master this information so you can use the manual to solve application errors on your own and come to me with programming errors.

19. *Employee:* I've got to do this?

Giving Good Data: Asserting Reflective Assumptions, Perspectives, Values

20. *Paul:* Yes. I expect you to examine how you do your work in an effort to improve how you do it, though until now I haven't provided you with adequate tools, and now I'm going to do that.

    (A long silence)

21. *Employee:* Have you considered that this may be beyond us, some of us, anyway?

Giving Good Data, Asserting a Search for Sense

22. *Paul:* No! The thought never crossed my mind. I'm off guard here. I understand this makes no sense to you and that you don't want to do it. But you're all capable of learning and using what I plan to teach you. Have you considered that you might be yanking my chain?

23. *Employee:* Paul, you're the fixer-*man!* We can't compete with you.

24. *Paul:* I'm not asking you to.

25. *Employee: You* don't think so. That's clear.

26. *Paul:* So, I'm not getting it? I should be concerned about your ability to learn? What are we talking about here: your sense of fear or inadequacy about learning the new material? [I was blindsided by the idea that they thought the material might be beyond them. It had never entered my mind. Once it had, I was torn: I didn't want to be played for a sap, and I didn't want to reject their apparent fear or sense of inadequacy out of hand. So I was pleased that I didn't automatically accept or reject this new thought. Instead, I tried to assert my sense making (in this instance, confusion) and inquire, without hiding either my doubt or my curiosity.]

27. *Employee:* I think so.

28. *Paul:* Really?

29. *Employee:* There are others who are concerned about this too. It's not just me.

30. *Paul:* That sounds very convenient, don't you think? Like "gathering friends" so I'll give this up? You see my problem.

31. *Employee:* Yeah, but no, I'm not pulling people out of the hat here. You're right, we don't want to do it. We want the fixer-man! But we're not sure we can do it either.

32. *Paul:* Help me out here, I'm not asking for names, but of the eight people out there, how many have you spoken with who've voiced a concern, you know—about "replacing" me?

33. *Employee:* That's it, Paul! That's how it feels to us! Like replacing you.

Listening

34. *Paul:* To me, it's just learning how to use the manual, but to you it's learning how to replace me?

35. *Employee:* Yep. Look, you're awfully good at it!

36. *Paul:* I know. But maybe I don't. I certainly haven't thought about the implication of that for you, for what I am asking of you now.

37. *Employee:* We're not dummies, but . . .

Giving Good Data: Asserting a Search for Sense

38. *Paul:* The irony is that I've been assuming *you* aren't and I am! *I've* been feeling like a dummy for expecting you to do something that I did not teach you how to do. By solving funny message problems myself rather than teaching you my skills and knowledge, haven't I kept you in the dark, perhaps contributing to your doubt about your ability to learn?

Outcome: Joint Invention of New Thinking and Behavior

39. *Employee:* That may be. I haven't thought about it. I like it when you do a fix. All of us do. It's great to have a Lone Ranger who rides to the rescue! Listen, if we've got to do this, let's at least do it in a group, not this one-to-one intensity. This promises to be a heavy load,

40. *Paul:* That's a reasonable request. But I'm famous for my soporific effect on groups, you know. I'd worry about putting everyone to sleep with material I need you to learn and use.

41. *Employee:* Well, then, keep the meetings short. Teach the "events," then have us bring the problems we have as we try to use them, so there's give-and-take instead of you doing all the talking.

42. *Paul:* That helps. We could meet for thirty minutes maybe once a week for three or four weeks and see how it goes. As you suggested, I could present event information at the first meeting; then the rest of the meetings would be give-and-take about how to use the information successfully.

43. *Employee:* Can you hold a meeting to thirty minutes?

44. *Paul:* No. You're right. But if you kept time . . .

45. *Employee:* Hey! Didn't I call about getting out of this?

46. *Paul:* I could sure use the help!

Commentary

Paul sets the context for interpersonal inquiry here by taking personal responsibility for a negative pattern in his behavior that contributes to the pattern of negative behavior by his employees. He is forceful in setting the reflective expectation that they will examine and take responsibility for their part in perpetuating the pattern. At the same time, he is no less forceful in his insistence on including himself (his own sense making) as part of the problem, expressed as a willingness to examine assumptions on which he has based the action he is taking here. He does not hide his blindness and consternation or his doubt and skepticism when the employee suggests an explanation for the employee's action that had never crossed his mind. He asserts his search for new sense, thereby inviting the employee to join him in trying to understand the situation and figure out a way to deal with it successfully. The employee accepts the invitation, and together they invent new thinking and behavior that might profit the employees in increased skill and Paul in decreased overload.

Like Paul, the lead character in the next and final story takes action in a way that demonstrates reflective communication to lead and learn. But he faces a sterner task, for he must begin by presenting an employee with information about a negative pattern in the employee's behavior, only to find that the employee does not see the pattern as negative. He sees it as positive. This is not peculiar but predictable in a pattern of negative behavior case and poses a special challenge to the skill repertoire of a leader who is committed to learning.

Story: Who Said I Go Overboard?

Mike, a platoon sergeant in the U.S. Army, demonstrates advanced use of reflective skills, sequencing all three skills in a variety of ways, masterfully improvising in an effort to engage Wayne, a squad leader, in interpersonal learning, and yet he fails. He shows us the limits of using learning skills with someone who does not buy the reflective approach and thinks the change he is being asked to make is dead wrong. Mike portrays his interaction with Wayne in both reflexive and reflective versions.[4]

Mike was in the U.S. Army. In recognition for outstanding performance as a squad leader, he was promoted to platoon Sergeant. As he had done while he was a squad leader, Mike prided himself in recognizing the differences and the possibilities in the various people in his platoon, treating each person fairly and equitably, and motivating each differently.

His superiors recognized Mike's work as superb, even though he had a different approach to managing people than the previous platoon Sergeant had. One of the squad leaders in Mike's platoon was Wayne. Mike and Wayne were squad leaders together before Mike was promoted to platoon Sergeant. Their superiors recognized that Mike and Wayne's styles complemented each other. Mike was thought to have a calming influence on Wayne, who was vocal and forceful. Wayne was often the leader Mike and others would turn to when it was time to get sixty people in order in a hurry.

Wayne's superiors decided that Wayne had pushed his approach to disciplining his men too far to the edge, becoming overbearing. His soldiers were complaining that they were treated harshly and unfairly held to higher standards than other platoons. Also, Wayne's superiors were concerned about Wayne's hot temper.

Mike was told to teach his management methods to Wayne so Wayne could break out of the overbearing nature of his style. Mike and Wayne had rarely talked about tough issues. When they had, it was with a great deal of sarcasm.

A Reflexive Interaction

1. *Mike:* Hey, Wayne, thanks for meeting me here off-duty.

2. *Wayne:* No problem. Any time. What's on your mind?

3. *Mike:* I'm just gonna come right out and say it. I've been hearing you're too hard on some people.

4. *Wayne:* Says who? Who's selling you this?

5. *Mike:* Never mind. Everybody knows you go overboard. (laughing)

6. *Wayne:* Who said I go overboard! My guys? What's this, a conspiracy? All I've been hearing are complaints, and now you! Who have you been talking to?

7. *Mike:* Everyone. I think everyone knows that you get crazy and start to yell.

8. *Wayne:* (interrupting) Everyone knows that you go too easy, and now you want me to do the same. I don't think so.

9. *Mike:* Just because I listen to what people say doesn't mean I'm easy.

10. *Wayne:* Okay, College Man. Trying out your theories on me? Hey, this ain't the Girl Scouts. People put their lives on the line. This is different from the corporate world. It's my responsibility to make sure things get done.

11. *Mike:* You never listen, do you? This has nothing to do with college. But speaking of which, you should try reading a book now and then. If you can.

12. *Wayne:* And then what? Know what you know? Do what you do? I don't think so. No one's walking all over me!

13. *Mike:* It's better than knowing squat and screaming your head off all the time!

14. *Wayne:* Is that what you think? Hey, people *listen* to me. Who do you ask to move people when they need moving? Me. You turn to me!

15. *Mike:* I don't turn to you to move anything! It's just that you're already yelling, and I ask you to include a few words that need to be said.

16. *Wayne:* Then ask me to step down. Is that what you want? If it is, then you've got it. I don't want to work for you anyway. Not if you're going to feed me this baloney!

17. *Mike:* Hey, calm down! No one is asking anyone to do anything here except to listen to me. You haven't heard one word I've said.

18. *Wayne:* (interrupting) Look, I gotta go. I'm done talking about this. Tell you what. My offer is on the table. If you want me to work elsewhere, I will. Go

for it. It's up to you. If you think you can run that platoon without me, then go for it. I'm outta here.

19. *Mike:* Maybe you should think some, too. Maybe some of what I told you will sink in through that hard head of yours. I'm not asking you to switch platoons!

20. *Wayne:* I'm done talking.

A Reflective Interaction:
Creating Conditions for Interpersonal Learning

First Meeting

1. *Mike:* Wayne, how are you?

2. *Wayne:* Fine. What's up?

3. *Mike:* In the past, when I've talked to you about your interactions with the men, we focused on an individual incident, like the Ames situation two weeks ago. Today is different. I hope we can look back over the time we've worked together and focus on a pattern I see in these incidents . . .

4. *Wayne:* (interrupting) What?

5. *Mike:* I just talked with the Captain and the First Sergeant. We all agree that it's important that I talk with you about a pattern in your behavior of angry hollering at the men that concerns us, and we hope concerns you . . . (Wayne starts to interrupt.) Hold it! Let me tell you what we talked about before you react. Sometimes you make it hard for a guy to get a word in edgewise. (Mike smiles nervously.) When I finish, you speak your piece. Then I hope we can talk about how we can both improve our leadership. I've got an hour now. We'll set up additional time when we stop. Sound all right to you?

6. *Wayne:* An hour?! This isn't going to be another of your college lectures?

7. *Mike:* No.

8. *Wayne:* Shoot! Go!

9. *Mike:* First, I want to tell you how much I value your hard work. I know you put your heart into what you do, and I appreciate you as someone I can count on when the chips are down. Second, you're invaluable in bringing the men to attention, order, and organization . . .

10. *Wayne:* (interrupting) Good thing there's someone who brings discipline around here! Now you drop the other shoe, right?

11. *Mike:* Not yet. I count on you to help me assemble the men in a hurry at opening formation. This is something you're much better at than I am. The Captain and the First Sergeant concur with these words of praise.

12. *Wayne:* Maybe you guys will see the light, yet . . . (Wayne appears ready to continue, but Mike interrupts.)

13. *Mike:* Let me paint the whole picture.

14. *Wayne:* Just heard the other shoe hit the floor.

15. *Mike:* The Captain, First Sergeant, and I see you angrily yelling at your men in front of the whole platoon in almost all of your contacts with them. Out of your squad of fifteen, six people have come to me with complaints, and I think more would come if they were not afraid. We're not talking one or two men here. And these six men are not your chronic bellyachers. They all have similar complaints: you embarrass them publicly with angry harangues, and you hold them to standards that are unreasonably high and unattainable. Because of this, their morale is low.

    What the First Sergeant, Captain, and I see as your hair-trigger temper is evident in other ways. Last month alone, you punched and broke that Jeep windshield because a column wasn't moving fast enough for you. Then you jumped all over Ames from Second Platoon because you thought he was on duty and in the wrong area, and it turned out he was in the right. I had all I could do to stop a fight between the two of you.

    Look, all of us need to find a balance between extremes of being too fearfully nice and too angrily tough. The Captain, First Sergeant, and I think you're at the too-angrily-tough extreme.

    What do you think about what I've said?

16. *Wayne:* I can't believe I'm in the Army, accused of being too tough on people!

17. *Mike:* So I'm talking nonsense?

18. *Wayne:* It isn't the Boy Scouts here. People should expect this to be a tough place. The work is tough. The people are rough. Lives are on the line. The men need me to get on them. You higher-ups are too easy on guys. That's when things get out of control.

19. *Mike:* So you bail us higher-ups out by screaming at the men?

20. *Wayne:* Well, sort of. Yes! You do go too easy on them. I'm not yelling just to yell. When there is a reason for me to motivate people, I speak up. Somebody has to!

21. *Mike: I'm* too easy on the guys , and you see your job as stepping in to discipline them for me?

22. *Wayne:* Yes. Right. When Murphy ran this platoon, things were different. I didn't have to yell as much. He did most of the yelling.

23. *Mike:* You wish things ran the way they used to?

24. *Wayne:* Yes. Very much so. I had no problems before you took over the platoon. Now I'm picking up the slack between what Murphy did and you don't do.

25. *Mike:* Wayne, I gotta back up. I'm knocked out by how strongly you believe we've lost our way here.

26. *Wayne:* Yes, indeed!

27. *Mike:* I'm wondering if I shouldn't give you information that has been kept private. It could explain — well, I'm not sure what it would explain, but at least you'd know what the higher-ups thought of Murphy's way of treating the men. I trust you will not repeat this information. It is confidential.

28. *Wayne:* I will not.

29. *Mike:* I believe you. Here goes. Because of personnel problems, Murphy was relieved of duty. He flew off the handle regularly. That is why they asked me to take over this platoon. He screamed at the men constantly, which resulted in poor morale. The Captain was tired of hearing complaints from Murphy's men. The First Sergeant was tired of the public displays that Murphy put on. After the blow-up at West Point in October, Murphy was given his walking papers.

    I know you don't know this, because we wanted to keep it low profile to protect Murphy's privacy. He was discharged because of this.

    As I listened to you, I thought that maybe we put you at a disadvantage by not including you in what happened and why. Had you known this, perhaps our expectations would have been clearer, and this conversation wouldn't have come out of the blue. I feel badly about that.

30. *Wayne:* I had no idea. You should have told me this before. I don't know what to say.

31. *Mike:* Does it make a shred of sense?

32. *Wayne:* I guess. Things are just falling apart. Murphy was a good man. He knew what these kids needed. I know he could get mean. Still, I'd have him over you college guys. You've got this all wrong. Just plain wrong.

    (A long silence ensues. Mike felt a door slammed in his face. His mind was blank, then filled momentarily with panic before he was able to quiet himself and continue.)

33. *Mike:* Just plain wrong? (Wayne is silent.)

    . . . We'll return to this . . . what? . . . impasse?

    Let's go back to the information I gave you before. I need to find out how you think about it.

I've received complaints from six of your men, each of whom has come forward separately. Six is pushing nearly half of your fifteen-person group. We're not talking one or two who are your chronic bellyachers. They all have similar complaints: you embarrass them publicly, and your standards are too high. Because of this, their morale is low.

Two weeks ago, in front of the entire platoon, you grabbed Harris by the collar and dragged him to the spot where you wanted him to be. Last week, you publicly humiliated Reynolds at Fort Drum with that personal matter that could have been better dealt with behind closed doors. What do you make of your behavior in these incidents?

34. *Wayne:* You're telling me to go easy on them.

35. *Mike:* I am not.

36. *Wayne:* Then you're talking in riddles.

37. *Mike:* "Going too easy on them" is not the only alternative to "going too hard on them." I'm looking for a balance between the two. For example, assuming you're not in an emergency situation, when you see a man making a mistake and he's thirty feet away from you, with the whole platoon standing between you and him, walk over and speak to him in a normal voice rather than screaming from where you are. (Wayne interrupts, but Mike keeps talking.) That's the kind of thing I'm talking about.

    Another example: when you discipline a man, you often put your nose against his as you shout or put your mouth against his ear when you shout. You can get the same result or better by standing back a foot or two, so the man doesn't feel violated by your invading his physical space. Also, rarely does a situation call for a squad leader to grab a soldier by the neck and drag him somewhere.

38. *Wayne:* You want me to be a pal to those thumb suckers!

39. *Mike:* No! Definitely not! I don't get it. What makes you so sure that I want you to pamper the troops?!

40. *Wayne:* Any time you need to get the platoon together, who do you look for to bust some ears?

41. *Mike:* That's it? Is that it? So you figure that shows I'm weak, so a weak guy like me could only want you to be weak and go easy on the men. Right?

42. *Wayne:* Right!

43. *Mike:* Well, you're right about me and tough discipline. It's not my strong suit, I agree. But what about the possibility that I'm strong, in that I can see you are better than I am at rousting and organizing the men, so I use that strength? None of us excels at every leadership task. What do you think?

44. *Wayne:* You college guys can talk your way out of anything.

45. *Mike:* Just blow smoke, huh?

46. *Wayne:* That's it.

47. *Mike:* I think your "college guy" slur is an easy dodge of a tough question. You're afraid to think about my question.

48. *Wayne:* Listen, everyone knows they send me the attitude cases. I'm supposed to straighten them out. It's been that way since I've been a squad leader. The First Sergeant assigns me all the crybabies. I'm not carrying tissues for them!

49. Wayne, you think the First Sergeant sends you all of the weaklings, the problem personnel, because he thinks you are the one to shape them up with your tough style?

50. *Wayne:* Right. Everyone knows that they send me the worst of the worst.

51. *Mike:* I'm trying to figure out how you got this information because it doesn't fit with what I know. (Wayne says nothing.) Did someone tell you this explicitly?

52. *Wayne:* Hey, it's common knowledge.

53. *Mike:* Wayne, the Captain and the First Sergeant don't send you all of the crybabies and problem personnel. For the past five years, we've been using a completely random assignment pool for new personnel. Not only that, but the Captain, the First Sergeant, and I feel that the problem people become problems after having been in your squad, in part because the only way you relate to them is through yelling at the top of your voice.

54. *Wayne:* That's a huge insult! I don't believe the First Sergeant said that stuff.

55. *Mike:* I don't like catching you off guard with this information. But he and the Captain will sit down with the two of us and repeat what I've just told you. We can walk to his office right now.

56. *Wayne:* Then why do I end up with the problem guys?

57. *Mike:* That's the right question. The answer is not that the First Sergeant sends them to you, as harsh as that might sound. It appears to us that you create them without meaning to and out of devotion to duty. With the best of intentions, your steady diet of angry, yelling behavior produces problem personnel. I want you to learn why this is happening and help you change it.

    Certainly I have learned through this conversation that I may have contributed to this pattern by not telling you about Murphy sooner. Trying to protect his privacy, we may have failed to set clear expectations for you. Also . . .

58. *Wayne:* (interrupting) *You* can change. That's fine. Not *me.*

59. *Mike:* I'm willing to look at my part in this. Maybe I need to change. But for today, though, our time is running out, so let's see if we can wrap this up. We're at an impasse: I think you need to learn and change, and you think I'm the problem in being too easy on the men? Right?

60. *Wayne:* You got it.

61. *Mike:* Before we stop, I'm going to repeat what I think we talked about, and I hope you will do the same. That way, even though the two of us don't agree, we'll both know better what our disagreement is about. Then I'll set a time when we'll get together the day after tomorrow.

62. *Wayne:* Not to waste more of my time, I hope.

63. *Mike:* Time will tell. Before we talked, I didn't know how poorly you evaluated my performance. I've got no credibility with you, right? (Wayne nods agreement.) That probably contributes to your finding it hard to believe what I've told you? I didn't know that you see yourself as the disciplinarian of the platoon of necessity because the Captain, First Sergeant, and I don't pull our weight as disciplinarians? (Mike waits for Wayne to nod before continuing.)

    I learned too that you think you were singled out for a special job here because of your abilities as a tough disciplinarian. That job was to take the worst of the worst and make them the best? (Wayne nods assent.)

    Finally, you may be puzzled about why it hasn't worked out that way — why your best efforts haven't made these eighteen-year-olds more orderly and responsible? (Again, Mike waits, but Wayne gives him a stone face. Wayne continues to sit, saying and showing nothing.) Am I getting it right?

64. *Wayne:* They're a bunch of crybabies.

65. *Mike:* I don't think so. For my part, I came to this conversation thinking you were the disciplinarian of the platoon not by choice or necessity, as you think, but by compulsion: you think that being a disciplinarian is the right way and only way. You don't have an alternative way.

66. *Wayne:* It is the right way.

67. *Mike:* I rest my case. I had no idea you thought you were chosen for a special assignment to shape up the riffraff. I feel badly about taking that honor from you, and yet that is the truth: you get recruits by random assignment.

    I'm troubled and will give thought to your observation that I, as well as the First Sergeant and Captain, fail to provide adequate discipline, relying too much on you, particularly at opening formation. I'll initiate talking further with you about this and talk with them.

Maybe we should have told you the facts about what happened to Murphy. Not having that information could have contributed to your thinking that your tough approach was what we expected here, but I doubt it.

What did you find out today? What sense do you take from our conversation?

68. *Wayne:* The Army's best days are behind.

69. *Mike:* That's discouraging to hear. Obviously I don't see it that way. I know you are devoted to your work and to the Army, and I want that devotion to pay off in today's Army. At the same time, you must know that you are headed down the Murphy path, and I hope you will stop now and make adjustments in your running of the platoon. I will help you if you are willing.

70. *Wayne:* And if I'm not willing?

71. *Mike:* I am sure you will seek a transfer, though that would be a mistake if you're looking for a career here, as I assume you are. You aren't going to find a lot of college guys like me who are willing to invest in you.

72. *Wayne:* This has been a waste of my time.

73. *Mike:* That's a shame. I want this to pay off for both of us.

Be here at 14:00 hours on Thursday.

Disheartening was the word for this conversation. My feelings were so mixed. It was quite confusing. I was repelled by and drawn to the guy. I wanted to shake his brains straight, and yet, through my exhaustion, I found myself liking and respecting him even more. I admired his resoluteness, his sense of duty, his straightforwardness with an occasional light touch, his cocky attachment to doing the right thing as he knew it. But also I hated his belligerent attachment to tough discipline as the only way and his blindness to being over the line in how he dispensed discipline. I wasn't after a makeover! An adjustment: that's what I wanted. He had so many good qualities that had a bad edge.

And he was right. I'm not a genius at tough discipline. Probably a reluctant C+. Given the choice, I prefer persuasion. His comments gave me pause. I wondered if he weren't right: maybe the college guys were weenies, undermining the fiber of American troops. But I was tired at the time. We weren't busting him for being a buster. We were busting him for being too much of a buster.

I talked with my superiors about Wayne's perception of us trading on his ability to roust and organize the men. Also, we talked about the inadvertent consequence of keeping the Murphy information from Wayne. That was certainly a lack of foresight for which we needed to take responsibility in planning our next action steps.

We discussed the possibility of my doing the rousting and organizing duties we had left to him, particularly at opening formation. I might gain credibility in his eyes, and at the same time find out if my taking the reins of discipline would free him to loosen his grip. This action step seemed worth the effort because we needed and wanted Wayne to change, and he seemed closed to seeing the need we saw. It had the advantage of our taking seriously his views of why he behaved as he did, and it put us in a position to find out if we were wrong about his current limitations, though I didn't think we were. Wayne and I met again three days later.

Second Meeting

1. *Mike:* Hi, Wayne. Did you have any further thoughts about our talk three days ago?

2. *Wayne:* Today, it's still a waste of time.

3. *Mike:* You see the need for me, the First Sergeant, and the Captain to be more forceful disciplinarians, thereby relieving you of some of that burden? More important, though, you'd see us doing more of what the recruits really need: tough discipline?

4. *Wayne:* Yes.

5. *Mike:* And you think that I'm letting the men down and the Army down by being too easy on the men? Right?

6. *Wayne:* Yeah.

7. *Mike:* So if you joined me in examining your screaming behavior, you'd be letting down the men and the Army — in effect, abandoning your own beliefs about right and wrong and about the duty you cherish?

8. *Wayne:* Exactly.

9. *Mike:* Obviously you and I are stuck. If you don't see the need for change that I do, we can't work together to make the change.

10. *Wayne:* Gotcha! Glad not to waste your time and mine.

11. *Mike:* So I've been thinking. What are our options here? I could toughen up my discipline of the men, particularly at opening formation. If I could, we could see if that gave you room to back off. (Mike waited to see if Wayne might respond, but he did not.)

    I talked with the First Sergeant and the Captain, as I said I would, about how you see us lacking tough discipline generally and particularly at opening formation. When I raised the idea of my taking the reins at opening formation to see if you could back off, they said fine. Also, we discussed our not telling you the reason for Murphy's discharge. They too wish we had found a way to include you so you would have better understood our expectations for how to handle the men.

12. *Wayne:* You can't do what needs to be done.

13. *Mike:* You don't trust that I could learn?

14. *Wayne:* Now that you put it that way. Right.

15. *Mike:* And I guess I don't think you could back off, even if I could.

16. *Wayne:* (smiling) Impasse?

17. *Mike:* Yep.

18. *Wayne:* (after a prolonged silence) I'll give you this. You aren't as bad a guy as I thought you were.

19. *Mike:* Yeah? Does that mean you'll work with me to try to figure out . . . (Wayne interrupts.)

20. *Wayne:* No, it means you're wrong, but you're not a jerk.

21. *Mike:* (laughing) Generous of you.

22. *Wayne:* Listen, you can't win me over by being a regular guy.

23. *Mike:* Well, I guess what I have to think about is whether I'm willing to toughen my behavior with the men, to see what happens and to see if I'm wrong about you. Maybe you can back off some?

24. *Wayne:* Who knows? But don't count on it.

25. *Mike:* Thanks for the tip. I'm doubtful that you could change because I think you've got an angry spot in you that drives you to do stupid things: yell constantly, smash a windshield, get in a fight. These are only the latest examples. You need to examine what's going on that drives you to do this stuff. Before we stop, I want you to have a picture of what we should do together twice a month. First, we need to focus on whatever your latest blow-up is with a man in your platoon, that is, go back through exactly what happened. Second, we need to talk about why you chose angry hollering to deal with the situation. What are your explanations? What are mine? That will get us into talking about anger: where it comes from and how to manage it. Third, I'll tell you alternative ways of handling the incident and ask you to practice them with me to see if you could build up a belief that they might work. Finally, you'd report back what happened when you tried something new. We'd talk about why it worked or didn't, see if we could improve on it.

26. *Wayne:* You must be dreaming!

27. *Mike:* Okay. I could order you to stop shouting.

28. *Wayne:* I would step down. Period. I'll go work elsewhere, I will.

29. *Mike:* Okay. We're going to try a four-week experiment. I'll take charge in opening formation to see if you can back off, bring your tone down a notch or two. Every Friday at 14:00 hours, we will meet for a half-hour, and you will give me feedback on my progress. I will give you feedback about whether I see you break the pattern of constant hollering at the men.

30. *Wayne:* It's your Army now.

My experiment was a long shot. I committed to it because it was my only shot.

Three weeks into this experiment, I was promoted and moved to a new division. In a good-humored way, Wayne told me that he hoped I'd learned something from him about how to be a better disciplinarian. I told him that I had. He declined my invitation for him to talk about what he might have learned with me.

I failed to engage Wayne as I had hoped. At the same time, perhaps I'd begun to build a foundation of trust and respect that could have led to our learning together. As we talked, we grew to respect one another. I felt this in our second conversation. His compliment, "You're wrong, but you're not a jerk," was a positive sign of trust and respect. The third time we met, he took delight in demonstrating proper disciplinary technique and insisted that I try it right there and then. Might the positive tone in his giving me feedback and instruction have led to his being more open to my feedback at some point? In the end, it is difficult to predict success from such inconclusive data.

Wayne's story ends sadly. Wayne's company (my company at the time of this story) was assigned to the Gulf War. They spent three months preparing for their trip overseas and waiting for orders to be shipped out. This was a stressful time for Wayne and his troops. What lay ahead added to the stress. Wayne's frustration level rose as he tried to keep his troops "in order" and "up to par." They were constantly disciplined by Wayne, and as they were, their morale dropped precipitously.

On their first combat mission, armed Iraqi troops surrendered to his platoon. Wayne grabbed and injured a soldier in his squad who was apparently not moving fast enough for him. As a result, Wayne was accused of "unacceptable conduct." He was reprimanded by his superiors, who had been watching his conduct closely for fear he would endanger people's lives. Two weeks after landing in Saudi Arabia, Wayne was relieved of duty.

Commentary

Unfortunately, for some people, the phrase *communicating to learn* means "we'll talk until we agree." The false hope is that interpersonal learning will bring unanimity and preclude the necessity for making the difficult decisions required by our position in an organization or family. Life is hard enough without false promises. So this chapter closes with a failure story to make the point that communicating to learn has its limits. Applying these skills does not automatically result in agreement or exempt us from our responsibility: we still have to exercise the courage to make difficult yet essential decisions about other people's performance.

We can only offer others the possibility and invitation to join us in reflective learning. We can create the conditions and make it attractive for them, but we cannot coerce them; they have to make the choice. In this story, Mike displayed remarkable skill at creating conditions for interpersonal learning, yet Wayne chose not to join Mike in reflective inquiry.

Wayne is the embodiment in dialogue of the hard-nosed manager sketched in the Introduction:

> He talks tough, and always thinks he is right, even when he doesn't know what's going on, blaming circumstances or other people. To him, the only alternative to in-charge decision making is wishy-washy weakness. He hates uncertainty, so takes action even when his ways of explaining things are inadequate. Feedback can only be an attack. Though he only talks and doesn't listen, he claims he does. He has no ability to engage other people in making new sense with him and figuring out what to do in difficult situations.

If we believe we hold the truth, as Wayne does here, then we feel no imperative to communicate to learn. Quite to the contrary, we feel an imperative to communicate to fix. Because we believe there is a fixed or static truth and we own it, it is self-evident to us that we should set right the people who are wrong (the people who make sense differently).

In the end, though, it is not Mike's failure that highlights his story; it is his courage and disciplined commitment to learning. He believes that investing in Wayne is his job and that creating conditions for interpersonal learning is the coin of that investment. He spends himself, so to speak, by:

- Laying the cards of his agenda on the table, though he knows it will be objectionable to Wayne

- Disclosing the bad news performance data nonjudgmentally and repeatedly (when Wayne refuses to address it) even though it baffles and infuriates Wayne

- Extending himself repeatedly in an effort to learn about and understand Wayne's different perspective, even though doing so is very painful

Though Mike repeatedly makes clear that the focus of these interactions is the need for Wayne to learn and modify his behavior, Mike insists as well that the interaction be two-way, not one-way. He pursues getting information from Wayne that predictably and painfully disconfirms his own view of his performance, and he does not do it pro forma.

When Wayne tells Mike in no uncertain terms that Mike is the real problem, not him, Mike does not retreat into private sense making, scheming, and the consequent behavioral manipulation that takes the form of the competition-for-listening pattern of interaction. He continues to disclose his surprise, consternation, and groping attempts to make new sense as invitations for Wayne to join him in a collective process of learning and change.

He questions his own definition of the problem as being Wayne's angry behavior, considering how his approach to disciplining the men might contribute to Wayne's excessive discipline. Even when Mike is at his wits' end and does not know what to do, he refuses to abandon his commitment to inventing new sense and behavior, as evidenced by his "four-week experiment."

In short, he reminds us of this description from the beginning of the book of a leader who integrates interpersonal learning and action:

> He talks sense, asserting himself when he thinks he is right *and* when he doesn't know what's going on or what to do. Confidently, he lays out his confusion and articulates messy situations, inviting his group to present new information, explanations, and feedback that he uses to question his own thinking, as well as theirs. He listens actively, sets out his reasoning, gives immediate feedback, synthesizes, and gets decisions made. Through interaction with him, people learn, change, and grow to be more productive.

Mike walks the talk and demonstrates a level of reflective skill that embodies the subtitle of this book: "Communicating to Lead and Learn."

The journey to this realm of action through the challenging process of discovery, invention, and practice is not easy, but it is vitally important. If you are willing, you can initiate the journey alone, though you will complete it only with others. Take the risk. Join those of us who look for company and help in expanding the community of people who are developing the ability to talk sense. You too will need help on your journey. Chapter Five provides that additional guidance.

Chapter Five

Along the Way: Further Guidance on Reflective Practice

The journey to change the way we communicate is a difficult one. Along the way, we get lost, and that is natural and inevitable, since the process of learning begins with questioning the very ground we stand on: our reflexive frame of reference. The result is doubt where before there was confidence. We are still constructing the alternative ground to step onto, in the form of a reflective frame of reference, and we are still authorizing the voice that can guide us forward.

Eventually the hope is that we will have confidence in this alternative ground and our reflective voice. Until then, we will at times need to regain our footing or renew our commitment to making the journey. This chapter is the place to come to for guidance. In a practical form, there are how-to guidelines and tips for learning and applying the reflective skills, as well as a discussion of the assumptions that underlie reflective practice. Answers are offered to questions that frequently arise as we develop a new reflective frame of reference and skills.

Step-by-step guidance is offered here in each of the four phases of the learning process: discovery, invention, practice, and action.

> **Discovery:** Here is a set of steps whose purpose is to create opportunities for discovering how our reflexive frame of reference shapes our thinking and consequent behavior.
>
> **Invention:** Here are the assumptions about people that are the foundation on which a reflective voice is constructed, contrasted with reflexive assumptions.
>
> **Practice:** Here are detailed practical instruction for producing the three interpersonal learning skills and using them together, as well as frequently asked questions (with answers) about learning the skills.
>
> **Action:** Here are more questions and answers that confront us when we apply reflective skills.

Discovery: An Exercise in Questioning the Ground You Stand On

The purpose of the analytical learning activity that follows is to create opportunities for discovery of your fix-it frame of reference. The exercise is best done with the assistance of a trusted partner, but you can also do the first eight steps alone if necessary. Think of the outline below as a skeleton, the full body of which is the "Triumph at Work, Trouble at Home" story. Rereading that story will enrich with detail the bare bones of this exercise and clarify how to proceed and produce useful results.

Remember that discovery can follow from direct analysis, as in the steps suggested below, but it also occurs as insight gained (often painfully) in the attempt to invent, practice, and act. This analytical exercise, though useful, cannot replace the learning you will gain through action, followed by feedback and insight.

An Analytical Exercise

Collecting Data for Discovery

1. Identify a difficult relationship and specific interactions.

2. Identify and write what the other person in the difficult interaction actually said. You can use Exhibit 5.1 on page 135.

3. Identify and write what you thought and felt.

4. Identify and write what you said in return.

Exhibit 5.1
Data Collection Form for Discovery Exercise, Steps 1–4

Directions: Recreate a minimum of three iterations of an exchange between you and the other person. You may need to collect data on as many as three different interactions to discover patterns.

Description of interaction:

What She/He Said	Your Thoughts/Feelings	What You Said
1.		
2.		
3.		
4.		
5.		
6.		
7.		

Analyzing the Information for Discovery

5. Examine this information for discrepancies that indicate the presence of your fix-it frame of reference:

   Assumptions about the other person: Is there information from which you can infer that you expect the other person to make sense the way you do? For example, do you find the other person's responses surprising and confusing because they are not what you expected or think they should be?

   Sense making: Is there information from which you can infer that your sense making is closed rather than open, and is there information to indicate that you view the other person as closed? For example, are you thinking and feeling judgmental, and do you see the other person that way?

   Behavior: Is there information from which you can infer that your behavior is controlled by an urge to fix the other person rather than create conditions for interpersonal learning? For example, does your behavior reflect a private agenda (a problem with the other person you see but have not talked about), information about your observations that you have withheld, or corrective behavior (criticism or reassurance) that you have directed at the other person instead of listening?

6. In the light of these discrepancies, consider the frame of reference embedded in your thinking, feeling, and behavior. Does the fix-it concept provide any useful explanation? Talk about and take notes on what you discover about the nature, implications, and limitations of relating to yourself and others through this frame of reference.

7. Predict the course of future interactions between the same parties. Will they be confined to the competition-for-listening pattern as they have in the past? Why or why not? What would give you hope for a break in the pattern?

Inventing New Thinking and Behavior

8. Invent and write new thinking and behavior for use in these interactions. In effect, script a new interaction. For example, in the interaction that you analyzed above, if the other person spoke first, write a new reflective response to that first statement. Then write the other person's second response, at once keeping the other person in character while allowing believable movement in response to your reflective inventions. Continue in this fashion until the conversation has run its course, or you get stuck. Use the practice sections in this book to guide the invention of new thinking and behavior.

Practicing New Thinking and Behavior to Enable Continuous Invention and Discovery

9. Practice new thinking and behavior in role=plays on videotape. Read from your scripts. Stop to talk about your internal reactions to reading from the script (it is one thing to write a script and quite another to look into someone's eyes and speak from it):

   - Initially you will be consumed by a sense of artificiality related to reading a script while being videotaped. Work through it. Keep reading.

   - You will be uncomfortable with your performance because of the formulaic and wooden nature of your scripted responses. Stop and adjust your responses to make them more natural and appropriate to the context.

   - You will get to the point where you can stop and talk about the deeper feelings and thoughts that emerge as you say things out loud that you have never before spoken.

   - Lots of questions and objections will emerge forcefully, and they are captured in the "Yes, But" sections in Chapter Four. Read those sections to comfort yourself by learning that other people have similar concerns. Expect that fear will be at the heart of most of your concerns and issues. Articulate these fears to your partner, and explore them. Stay open to the possibility that experiencing these fears is analogous to what happens when you leave home for the first time: though freeing, the departure can be quite frightening as well. Your home has been your fix-it voice, and you are saying things on tape that make no sense from that frame of reference because your responses violate sacred assumptions. These unarticulated assumptions constitute the unquestioned ground of your fault-finding, fix-it frame of reference. Formulate these assumptions verbally and in writing.

10. Watch the tapes. When you see yourself do something that stings you, stop the tape, and force yourself to articulate and explore the explosion of thought and feeling. Again (once you get past a cosmetic viewing of yourself on tape), assume that you are probably frightened because the behavior you are trying to produce on tape tacitly questions the unquestioned ground on which you have always stood. Articulate tacit assumptions, and write them down.

11. Ask for feedback about the relationships between what the other person said, how you thought and felt in response, and what you said in return. Stay open to insight into the workings of your fix-it thinking and feeling and your reflexive voice.

12. Reverse roles in the role playing so both parties can feel and discuss the different consequences of new and old behavior. Exchange feedback about the relationships between what the other person said, how you thought and

felt in response, and what you said in return. Stay open to insight into the workings of your reflexive voice.

Commentary

The discrepancies cannot be discovered readily through abstract analysis or contemplation of how we think we would handle difficult encounters. Such thinking, done outside the context of eye-to-eye interaction, seldom yields new knowledge of our own discrepancies because discrepancies appear when we are unsettled by the emotional electricity that jolts us on hearing information we do not want to hear or giving information we do not want to give. Discrepancies are revealed when the interpersonal encounter is charged with the voltage of different information and different interpretations of the information, as most important encounters are.

Just because discrepancies show themselves in these charged situations does not mean we can gain awareness of them readily, let alone accept them as our own. After a jolting interaction, it is hard to remember what happened, let alone reflect on our actions to discover that we didn't do what we thought we did. A woman who had just viewed her handling of a tough interaction on videotape spoke for all of us when she said, "I didn't do what I planned, and I didn't remember what I did!" Reviewing the tape, she gradually laid claim to being where she actually was but did not want to be: much less skilled than she thought.

Year after year, we are likely to be surprised by the number of times we rediscover that:

- We assume that others are or should be making sense the way we are.

- We think we are open to change in our sense making (though we are actually closed) while the other person is closed.

- We behave to fix things while advocating learning.

This pattern of repeated discovery can produce awe, but it can also be discouraging because it is a reminder that we are not where we think we are. At times, discouragement is accompanied by anger and a sense of defeat and hopelessness. Our tendency is to run from these feelings in denial (flight) or harangue ourselves (fight) because their existence is proof that we have failed in our quest to get located. Discovery is the act of getting located, and we make it a goal to be achieved in our quest, so when repeated insight reminds us that we are not there, we react in a reflexive flight-or-fight way. We can break this pattern by thinking about our feelings from the reflective perspective that they are proof of failure only within a reflexive perspective. Reflectively, they are evidence of caring and courage to learn and can be accepted as such. When they are, we can come through them, as we would a door, into the invention of a new assumption: that getting located is not a once-and-for-all act but part of an ongoing process of continuous growth toward humility and wisdom.

Invention: Contrasting Reflexive and Reflective Assumptions About People

Invention is about creating an internal voice that is committed to and capable of guiding us toward making communication an act of interpersonal learning. It begins with basing our integrity in a new set of assumptions—a set of reflective rather than reflexive assumptions about people.

You may want to reread the "So I'm Not Stupid?" and "Triumph at Work, Trouble at Home" stories in Chapter Two, paying attention to the reflective assumptions and perspectives that are presented there, particularly in the consultant's internal dialogue in "Stupid" and the explicit explanations of the consultant's actions in "Triumph."

Presented here in greater depth, the following assumptions about people are the foundation on which a reflective voice is constructed.

People Are Sense Makers, Not Repositories of the Truth

Inside a reflexive frame of reference, we hold ourselves to this expectation: people should have sense made, once and for all. In a reflective mode, we wish we always had sense made but we do not expect it. Sense made is a goal but not an expectation, so we are compassionate with ourselves rather than disheartened when events throw us into sense-making soup. We feel pride in our ability to navigate the unruly seas of sense making, as painful as the turbulence can be.

Inherent in being a sense maker is a need to make sense of our own lives, though, paradoxically, we cannot make sense alone, for we are social beings. Trust (or lack of it) in our ability to make new sense reflects the nature of our interactions. Reflexive interactions teach us to trust other people's either-or sense making, while reflective interactions support us in wrestling new sense from our experience and thereby gaining trust in our own ability to make new sense.

People Are More Than Their Behavior

We are often frustrated by what other people do because we are inside the reflexive frame: people are their behavior.

If people are only their behavior and its results, as we often think, then it makes absolutely no sense to listen for understanding (to give only one example of a reflective skill). It is nonsensical. What makes sense is to correct for improvement. This activity takes little conscious effort because we are reflexively equipped to correct by criticizing or reassuring.

In contrast, if people are their behavior and its results and also their intentions, efforts, needs, values, beliefs, hopes, feelings, expectations, ideas, and sense making, then it makes sense to listen for understanding. It is nonsensical not to listen for understanding because not to listen would be to refuse to relate to people.

People Are Multiple Selves

We are often frustrated when people say one thing and in the next moment say something different because we are inside the reflexive frame that people should speak from a single voice.

In fact, we have multiple selves or different voices. Only moments after we speak in one voice adamantly advocating the need to accept a new job offer at twice the salary, another voice within us says, "Wait a minute! I'm not so sure I want to give up my seniority. My husband loves his job. Our youngest child has one more year in high school." Then the original voice speaks back: "But this is a once-in-a-lifetime career opportunity!"

The back-and-forth exchange continues, arguing opportunity against security, self-interest against the interests of others, each voice presenting arguments based on different values or principles. As we make decisions, this kind of exchange occurs constantly.

Another way to say that we are multiple selves is that people are ambivalent by nature.[1] Ambivalence is not something we grow out of as we get older. To the contrary, as we mature, we become more comfortable with our ambivalence.

Throughout our lives, we want to be predictable and unpredictable, simultaneously. We want to be secure and adventurous, enjoying the benefits of certainty and tasting the excitement of the unknown. We yearn to care for others, while at the same time we want to be taken care of by others. We want to make sense of our own lives, and we want answers from authorities.

Each of us prefers a different degree of balance between these inherent tensions, but none of us is free of them.

People Are Chains of Meaning

We are often frustrated, angered, and feel under attack when people respond harshly to us because we are inside the reflexive frame (people are logical and should behave so).

Actually, people's insides are organized not logically but psychologically. Ideas, feelings, images, and experiences are linked together in ways that cannot be predicted by logic from inside our own frame of reference. For example, a woman says to her husband, "Don't forget to put gas in the car." Knowing his pattern of forgetfulness about daily things, she sees herself as going out of her way to be helpful, so she predicts logically that he will say, "Thanks. I wouldn't want to run out of gas with a new client in the car." In fact, "Get off my back!" is his harsh response.

How might that response be explained? Inside all of us, ideas, feelings, images, and experiences are as links in a chain, interconnected. If a single item in the chain is mentioned, all flash on instantaneously, like the bulbs in a string of holiday lights, imbuing the single item with all of the interrelated meanings. The husband might respond as he did because of the chain of meanings he sees connected to the wife's comment: "She's criticizing me again." (linked to) "She always treats me like a child!" (linked to) "If I allow her to treat me this way, it will confirm my worst fear that I am incapable of taking care of myself!"

Chains of Interlocking Meanings

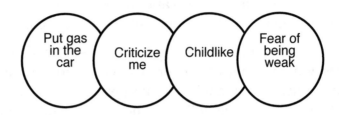

People Yearn to Be Whole, But Often Expect to Be Perfect

Reflexively, our model for growth is perfection. Reflectively, our model for growth is wholeness.[2]

In the story "So I'm Not Stupid?" Ben cares for himself through a reflexive frame of reference, treating himself as a problem to be solved. He sees himself as in a toxic place (no sense) that he needs to get out of. His sense-making effort takes the form of fight or flight:

- Fight: "Well, what's wrong with me?!" he demands of the consultant, apparently demanding a quick fix.

- Flight: "Yeah, but how do I get out of this mess?" he asks the consultant, hoping to flee from his uncomfortable stuckness.

Tacitly he is relating to himself through the common form of an if-then equation: "If I can get rid of this unwanted presence [stuckness in this instance], Then I can . . . [feel better or think better, for example]."

This if-then equation is the operational form of a perfection model of human growth. Like Ben, we expect that people should be perfect.

The contrasting reflective assumption is that people yearn to be whole though often expect to be perfect. When we act from our yearning to be whole instead of an expectation to be perfect, we assume that inclusion is the pathway to growth. So we work to welcome into full participation within ourselves all of our different parts or voices: feelings, wishes, images, thoughts, and conditions such as searching for sense and no sense. The imperative for growth is this: "If I can risk feeling my feelings or accepting myself as flawed, for example, then I can relate rationally and not defensively to other people who present me with their feelings, flaws, and so on."

The very parts or voices we seek to welcome when inside a reflective model are those parts or voices we attempt to exclude within a reflexive model because the goal of growth is to be perfect, not whole. Our effort is to expunge unwanted parts or voices in pursuit of perfection. The imperative for growth is this: "If I can get rid of my shortcomings and imperfections or my feelings of anger, for example, then I can be competent as a boss, a parent, a friend."

Internally, if we are trying to rid ourselves of our "bad" or "shouldn't be" parts, whether they are anger, fear, confusion, no sense, ambivalence, or uncertainty, then we will act interpersonally to rid other people of their "bad" parts that we believe will keep them from attaining perfection.

In contrast, if we pursue becoming less fearful of our own fear, anger, or grief; more welcoming of the conditions of searching for sense or no sense; more aware and accepting of our yearnings to be taken care of, then we will be less likely to react with defensiveness when we are in the presence of other people who are in fear, or no sense, or in need of help. Unafraid of fear in ourselves, we no longer fear it in others. Accepting of the condition of no sense in ourselves, we can be accepting of it in others.

People's Defenses Are Experienced as Their Integrity

When we offer help to a child, friend, client, employee, or boss, we often cannot make sense of why they receive it as a hindrance.[3] Our positive efforts are ignored, merely tolerated, or may even yield an outburst or the freeze. Often we think or say, "Don't be so defensive! I was just trying to help," because we are inside the reflexive frame: people should not be defensive, people should be receptive.

- In "A Son Drops Out of College," the son's flight from home makes no sense to his parents, who were trying to help him when he fled.

- In "The Cord of Wood," June's laconic, ambivalent response to Terry's offer of the firewood makes no sense to Terry, who was trying to help her enjoy the house.

- In "Million Dollar Listening," the client's repeated request for a simulation makes no sense to the owner, who repeatedly offered helpful explanations and demonstrations to answer the request.

The parents, Terry, and the owner expect their help to be received, only to have it rejected. So they label the other people's behavior as defensive. The son's flight; June's laconic, ambivalent response; and the prospective client's repeated request are given a negative valence.

Ironically, these same behaviors, as experienced from within, often carry a positive valence: the son is extricating himself from an unreceptive interaction; June is protecting herself from a rental agent she thinks is reneging on his verbal contract; the prospective client is persisting in an effort to get his needs recognized. In effect, behavior that we see as other people's defensive fight-or-flight moves, they often see oppositely as expressions of their integrity.

Of course, the same behavior can be at once defensive and an expression of integrity. The name we place on the behavior governs how we respond to it. If we name the behavior *defensive,* we have made it a deficiency that we feel responsible to correct. If we name the behavior an *expression of integrity,* we have made it a legitimate quality of a person. As such, we feel responsible to show honor and respect through an act of inquiry: What might be at stake for this person? On the receiving end, the difference between "Why are you being so defensive?" and "Tell me about the urgency?" can be the difference between a slap in the face and an invitation to be known.

Practice: How-To Instruction on the Reflective Skills

Here you will find both detailed practical instructions for producing the three interpersonal learning skills and using them together, as well as frequently asked questions (with answers) about practicing the skills. Often people need these questions answered before they are comfortable proceeding.

When you are practicing the skills, you may want to reread the three skill "Concept" sections in Chapter Three. As an exercise, try rereading "The Cord of Wood," "Are You Calling Me a Liar?" (reflective version), and "They Come Back with the Same Problems" stories, focusing your attention on the internal monologues explaining the characters' struggle to produce reflective thought and behavior.

How to Structure: Guidelines and Tips

1. *Remember the punch line.* Good structure creates the conditions for good talk and good listening.

2. *Distinguish method from purpose.* When preparing to present negative information to someone, clarifying the real purpose will be the most difficult part. People often confuse method (how the interaction will occur) with purpose and outcome. For example, a common opening statement meant to

clarify purpose or outcome is, "I've asked you here to discuss what went on with Bob." But "to discuss" is not a purpose; it is a vehicle or method. A discussion is aimed at achieving something—for example, clarity about the issues, change in behavior, or invention of a set of options.

When you think you have your real purpose clear, write it down or say it out loud, as if speaking directly to the person. Then ask yourself: "Am I talking about the outcome I expect (purpose) or about how I plan to get there (method/procedure/steps)?"

3. *Practice an opening statement.* Write out an opening statement with the plan you want to propose. Expect that you will have difficulty constructing a statement that communicates real purpose, procedure, and time period; is short rather than long; and is colloquial in language rather than formal.

When you have written a draft opening statement, ask yourself, "How will the receiver respond?" Most likely, your answer is this: "Defensively!" This is particularly true if the anticipated conversation involves giving negative information or asking for a change in the other person's behavior. If you anticipate a defensive response from the other person, you may err and withhold the real purpose, figuring that you can work around to it indirectly. Predictably, the receiver will return the favor, acting from the same indirectness by psyching out what is really going on and responding with protective or defensive gaming.

It is not always possible or advisable to state the real purpose early in an interaction, and it is often hard to accomplish. Still, you can handle anticipated defensiveness from the receiver not by keeping your real purpose to yourself but by preparing yourself to listen to the receiver with empathy in a spirit of openness.

4. *Use joint inquiry instead of Twenty Questions.* When people come with problems, instead of launching into a series of questions, tell them a methodological set of steps you want them to try with you, or simply give them a written list of the questions that embody the steps. Use the method or list of questions to guide your joint inquiry into the problem. After arriving at a solution, review the method and talk about how they might use it on their own or with others.

For example, a manager might say to a supervisor, "Before we close, how did using the three-step method of reconstructing what you've tried, analyzing why your efforts haven't worked, and then inventing and role-playing the new approach work for you? It's worth talking about for two reasons: so you and I can improve the process and so you might use it when your reports come to you with similar problems. It's important to me that we teach our people problem-solving methodologies rather than solve their problems for them because we want them to expand their skills rather than repeatedly turn to us for solutions."

5. *Stay in charge of the structure.* After gaining confidence in how and when to structure at the beginning of an interaction, the next challenge is to use the problem exploration steps to guide the interaction. Avoid both the reflexive tendency to forget the steps entirely when the conversation begins or to insist on their use even if they aren't working. Guidelines for staying in charge of a structure are stated below, along with examples.

A manager has a problem with one of his supervisors. He comes to the general manager to discuss it. The general manager takes the lead in structuring: "Let's try this: I'll help you recall what you've done to try to solve this problem and take notes so we're sure we're looking at the same thing. With that history in front of us, we'll stop and analyze why these efforts haven't worked. Finally, we'll use our analysis to invent a new approach. What do you think?" The manager responds, "Sounds good to me." As the two managers proceed, the general manager would stay in charge of structuring the interaction, following the guidelines below. Each guideline is illustrated by an example.

Guideline 1: When you complete one problem-solving step, say so explicitly. Check for agreement with the other person, and name the second step before acting on it.

Example: "I think we've recreated a list of your attempts to solve this problem. I'll read back through my list. After you've confirmed the list, we'll see if we can figure out why your efforts didn't work."

Guideline 2: When you are not sure where you are relative to the steps in your plan, stop, say so, and ask for help in relating the current conversation to the plan.

Example: "I'm at a loss about how the last five minutes of discussion relate to our objective of analyzing to see why your efforts failed. Are we off track?"

Guideline 3: When you see that both of you have abandoned the structure, say that you see this has happened. Check to see if the other person agrees, and explicitly state whether you think the two of you should return to the plan or let it go and set a new next step.

Example: "I think we've abandoned the steps in how we planned to proceed. Do you? If so, let's step back and figure out why and where to go from here."

Guideline 4: When you discover that you began the interaction with inferences or assumptions that are questionable, identify them explicitly. Talk about any implications for redefining the purpose of the interaction or the nature of the problem under discussion. Then restructure in a way that fits the new definitions.

Example: "You've given me a great deal of information I didn't have when we began. At the beginning of our conversation, I assumed this was an interpersonal problem between you and your supervisor. Now I'm questioning that assumption and wondering if there isn't a larger organizational issue at the center of this. For me, that implies scrapping the problem-solving steps we'd planned and instead trying to figure out how to get information that will confirm or disconfirm that we have an organizational problem. What do you think?"

Guideline 5: When you have gone through an agreed-on problem-solving sequence and come to a problem definition or solution, say so explicitly. Check to see if the other person agrees; bring closure explicitly and move on.

Example: "Are we in agreement that what we have is an organizational problem? If so, let's move on to develop alternative ways of solving it."

Paradoxically, staying in charge of the structure does not preclude the other person from being in charge too. The whole point of having a clear and shared structure is to allow for mutual control.

6. *Explicitly state your rationale when structuring.* Tell the people who normally come to you for help that you are going to try to clarify the purpose of your interactions with them before you react with an answer. Then when someone comes to you, experiment with asking questions to clarify the purpose of the interaction before offering help in your reflexive problem-solving mode—for example:

- "Are you looking for my answer or help in thinking this through?"

- "You want a sounding board? My solution? Something else?"

- "Are you looking for an answer from me, or is this for your information, or are you looking for me to be a sounding board?"

If the purpose is thinking through, then use learning skills. If the purpose is problem solving, do that. If the purpose is for information, clarify the information.

Initially you and others might be confused as you make the transition from your reflexive problem solving to reflectively clarifying the purpose of the interaction before getting into it. After several attempts, seek feedback from people who come to you: "You know, I've gotten feedback about too quickly giving answers to people's questions. I'm trying to change that by stopping to clarify the purpose of an interaction before I respond." Then ask:

- "How did the interaction go for you?"

- "Did you get what you needed?"

- "How could I better help you get what you need?"

Stay alert for feedback that is given spontaneously, such as,

- "Thanks, I appreciate the help in thinking this through."

- "It was good to bat this around. Thanks."

- "The give-and-take is what I needed! Thanks for holding your fire."

Do not discount such feedback out of ignorance and disbelief by saying:

- "What! I didn't even do anything!"

- "All I did was listen."

- "You came up with the answer by yourself!"

7. *Improvise as necessary.* The best-laid plans must be put aside or revised. For example, when confronted by persons who are beside themselves, stop structuring and start listening to understand. When you think the other person feels heard, try to set the structure. If the person does not join in setting the structure, listen again before structuring.

Developing good judgment about when to press, when to let go, and when to revise your structuring statement takes time and practice.

How to Give Good Information: Guidelines and Tips

1. *Remember the punch line.* You need to give good information to get good information.

2. *Draft "When, I Feel, Because" statements until they're nonjudgmental.* Few of us realize how judgmental our thinking and behavior are when we are involved in an interaction that matters to us. Writing a feedback statement before giving it reveals the judgmental nature of our thought.

Here is a typical first draft of a feedback statement written by an employee to her boss: "You shouldn't ask me for work on the day you want it. It's not right because you need to plan better and think about your employees."

The writer felt very strongly that this "When, I Feel, Because" statement met the criteria for effectiveness, and on questioning by colleagues, denied that it was in any way judgmental. Yet this first draft is not effective: the "when" part does not provide observable data, the "I feel" part is not a statement of feeling, and the "because" part blames the receiver rather than presenting the impact on the speaker. In addition, the draft uses highly judgmental language such as "shouldn't ask," "It's not right," and "you need to plan better and think about your employees." On a school grading scale, it would be an F.

Here is a fourth draft of the original: "Last week, on Thursday, at noon, you asked me to prepare the retrofit analysis and narrative for a three o'clock meeting that day. I was frustrated because, being unfamiliar with the narrative portion of the report, I could not prepare it as thoroughly as I would have liked in that time period. It was an eight-hour job done in three hours, so did not show the quality of work I take pride in."

This fourth draft came after forty-five minutes of intense exchange between the writer and three of her colleagues. This writer, like most of us, found it hard to extricate herself from reflexive blaming. Yet eventually she learned the discipline of giving good data and broke the competition-for-listening pattern.

3. *Use specific, concrete, quantifiable data in the "when" part of your statement.* When writing or giving the "when" part of the statement, we often err by presenting abstract or inferential or emotionally laden information instead of giving observable information. Read the following first draft of the "when" part of a feedback statement and grade it on an A-to-F scale for meeting the criteria of specific, concrete, quantitative (observable information): "Whenever we meet and I ask you for a decision about the merchandise, you always put off making a decision."

After fifteen minutes of questioning from colleagues, the writer redrafted her original statement, replacing all her abstractions and inferences with observable data: "We have been meeting together twice a week since April 1. It is now June 15. By my calculations, we have met approximately twenty times. At each of these meetings, I have asked you for a decision regarding what merchandise to order, and you have said you would let me know. To date, I still do not have a decision from you."

It's revealing to see the events behind the inferential, emotionally laden language of the first draft. Contrasting the redraft with the original, it should be clear that the original receives a grade of F.

4. *Explicitly state your emotional reaction in the "feeling" part.* People often omit the feeling statement entirely because they assume feelings have no place in business. This is a controversial assumption. From a reflective practice perspective, it is not a question of whether feelings are part of the workplace. They are. The question is: How can people take responsibility for their feelings and manage them appropriately in the workplace? The danger in

omitting the "I feel" part is that it greatly increases the likelihood that the language and undertone of the whole statement will be judgmental and blaming.

Often when people try to explicitly state their feelings, they err in mistaking a thinking statement for a feeling statement. Consider the following example: "When . . . , *I feel you are always* . . . , because . . . " "I feel you are always" is not an explicit statement of feeling. It simply uses the word *feel*. An explicit statement of feeling would be, "I am angry" or "I am upset." Another common example of stating a thought as a feeling is: "When . . . , *I think it would be* . . . , because . . . "

To make the "feeling" part of your statement effective, check that you are using a word that specifically describes your emotional state. Also strive to accurately convey the intensity of your emotion: Are you "bothered"? "frustrated"? "angry"?

5. *Present the cause-and-effect relationship between the "when" and "because" part of your statement.* If you are working in an environment that is hostile to explicit expressions of feeling, you may choose to omit the feeling statement intentionally. Consider the following "When, I Feel, Because" statement: "Today at the first staff meeting, you joked twice and interrupted me twice. That upset me because I couldn't get through the last three items of my agenda." The key cause-and-effect relationship is between the joking and the interruptions and not getting through the last three items on the agenda. This key relationship can be communicated without including the information about being upset.

6. *State the impact on you, the speaker, in the "because" part.* People err in the "because" part by stating the impact statement on the person spoken to rather than showing the impact on you, the speaker. For example, here is a boss talking to an employee (the "Because" is in italics): "When you arrived at yesterday's staff meeting a half-hour late, *it was unfortunate because we have talked about this before: you do not plan your time properly.*"

The "because" part of this example incorrectly aims the impact at the listener. Instead, the "because" part should reveal the impact on the speaker (and others). Rewritten correctly to show the impact on the speaker, the draft above might read: "When you arrived at yesterday's staff meeting a half-hour late, I was upset because you had the report we were scheduled to discuss, so ten of us had to kill a half-hour and suffer two costs: one was financial—about $500 in payroll—and the other was a loss of opportunity for all of us to work those five hours on other projects."

7. *State the impact in concrete time and money terms in the "because" part.* Often the "because" part of the statement is too general and abstract. Instead, state the impact in time and money terms using specific, concrete, quantitative language. Consider the following example: "When . . . , I was pleased with your preparation work and presentation because it added so much to the meeting and made a great impression on the board."

General language of this kind ("added so much to the meeting" and "great impression") has only momentary positive impact on the receiver's morale. It does not help the receiver know what he or she did, so the receiver might repeat it by choice. In addition, the general language does not help set expectations concretely through giving positive feedback. Rewritten to give a more specific, concrete presentation of the actual impact, the "because" part of the statement reads: "Your presentation was short (only five minutes) and to the point (three decision items). Your backup information was both comprehensive and detailed, offering price ranges for Alpha, Vax, and, where possible, PC platforms. Given only two days to complete this project, you performed above my expectations. You made our department budget report more convincing, and the board chairperson told me your report helped the board focus its decision making!"

A related error in the "because" part is when the speaker presents only the psychological impact on himself or herself. Instead, strive to state the impact in time and money terms. Two examples of speakers who incorrectly state only psychological impact follow: "When . . . , I was . . . , because the clients will think worse of me" and "When . . . , I am . . . , because it makes me lose confidence in my work."

In general, avoid giving psychological impact. Granted, if trust is high and both people are skilled, stating psychological impacts can contribute to learning. But otherwise the result is the competition-for-listening pattern, hurt feelings, and misunderstandings. Instead, analyze a first draft statement in an effort to turn it toward actual costs. If it cannot be done, consider not giving the feedback unless there is a very high degree of trust between the people exchanging the information.

8. *Use the "When, I Feel, Because" format when giving both positive and negative feedback.* This format works equally well when the speaker wants to reinforce praise or reprimand people. It makes your response to their behavior explicit and concrete. This format is also useful in setting clear and concrete expectations for performance in the context of what someone has actually done. Setting expectations in the context of actual performance increases the likelihood that people remember them rather than put them in the circular file with the rest of the generally stated expectations.

150

9. *Practice first with positive feedback: give observable data along with inferences.* To start getting used to this format of giving good data, use the "When, I Feel, Because" format for giving positive feedback once a week for three months with each of your key people. It will improve morale and productivity. People like to be told when they are doing a good job and want to know clearly and concretely what their boss expects so they have a fair shot at meeting or exceeding those expectations.

A positive feedback statement serves as both a pat on the back and a task-oriented presentation of what matters to the speaker. Here is an example of a boss presenting positive feedback to an employee in the "When, I Feel, Because" format: "Sue, when you offered such a useful explanation of the Quark user problem that Aldona was having on Tuesday this week and then stayed to helped solve the problem, I was grateful for several reasons: you demonstrated initiative and a willingness to make helping others a priority, even when it wasn't convenient and when you were on a tight deadline of your own. You saved us hundreds of dollars in potentially lost staff hours, searching for an understanding of the problem. In the end, not meeting that 7:00 P.M. deadline on Tuesday could have cost us a contract!"

10. *Give negative feedback about patterns of behavior differently from single-incident feedback.* "When, I Feel, Because" is a useful format for giving single-incident feedback but inadequate to giving feedback about patterns of behavior that have persisted over time. You must do data collection and analytical work prior to talking about a pattern, with the result of naming the pattern, identifying two or three concrete examples, quantifying the number of sources (across constituencies) and a range of the number of repetitions of the pattern in a given time period. (See the second version of the "Are You Calling Me a Liar?" and "Who Said I Go Overboard?" stories for examples of pattern data presented in this form.) You must do this preparation work in order to communicate the significance of the data.

You cannot present pattern data an incident at a time because the other person will address each incident with part of the truth, and when you stop, you will be no further than you were at the outset. Anticipating this, you must say something to this effect before giving examples: "The message here is in the whole, not the sum of the parts, so please let me get through all of the examples. Then let's talk about the pattern." Then, during the exchange, you must be disciplined in refocusing the discussion on the whole after listening to the other person's explanations of why individual incidents occurred.

11. *If you give negative feedback, expect to get it in return.* You cannot give negative feedback without getting it in return. When you do, you will feel under attack and attribute conscious negative intent to the other person, naming him or

her as defensive. These reflexive feelings and thoughts are not necessarily correct. (You will feel that you must get the other person corrected first, before you can entertain what came back to you in return.) The other person may indeed be responding defensively and yet simultaneously giving you information that you need to learn, grow, and change. You can choose to listen and respond not to the defensiveness you see out there but to the negative information about you, and then explore it for the purposes of your own learning.

As a consequence of reflectively taking responsibility for your own learning, you will be modeling what you hope the other person will be willing to do in response to the negative feedback you gave. However, modeling is not your purpose. It is a consequence of your purpose, which is learning.

After listening and exploring the negative data about you, reassert the negative feedback you gave at the outset and ask the other person to use it as a catalyst for reflection and possible change.

12. *Assert your search for new sense by using a sequence of steps.* Let's say that you receive negative information that disrupts the sense you had made of some situation. "Oh, no!" you say to yourself. You recognize your reflexive tendency to hide your bafflement and sense your ambivalence about including another person in a search for new sense:

Step 1: Remind yourself about reflective assumptions. Help yourself choose to go public with your sense making, rather than stay private by saying to yourself something on the order of:

- "Leadership is not having answers alone but exercising a repertoire of ways to find answers with other people."

- "I can empower people to trust their own sense making by being a leader who makes sense with them instead of a person who makes sense alone and announces only the products of that sense making. By announcing only the products of my sense making, I teach people what a good problem solver I am. As a result they will keep coming to me for answers. Actually, my goal is to enable them to become better and more confident problem solvers. To accomplish the goal, I must take the risk of asserting my sense making."

- "I can be at loose ends in my thinking and behave competently as an interpersonal learner."

Step 2: Be explicit about where you are in your sense making: "I'm trying to make sense of this," "I'm confused," or "I'm at a loss about how to explain what's going on." Disclose the bits and pieces in your mind that don't add up; try to articulate what information doesn't fit with what other information. Then structure by declaring the purpose, procedure, and time period (if appropriate) for inquiry or decision making.

Step 3: Be explicit about the kind of help you need. Tell others what kind of information would be useful for you to hear from them.

- Others often present conclusions without the reasoning that leads to them. Without access to the reasoning, you cannot trust the conclusions. So say, "I can see you feel strongly about X. Help me understand the thinking that led you to X, will you?"

- Others often offer inferences without the observational information from which the inferences were derived. Without the observations, you cannot trust the inferences. So say, "Will you try to recall for me what occurred that led you to think that?"

- It will not be easy for people to give good observational information because observation, feeling, and consequence get whooshed together in the mind, then expressed often as judgmental inference or conclusion. You will have to help people separate one kind of information from another, gradually reconstructing what happened.

Step 4: Listen reflectively to what people say. Listen motivated by the idea that important feedback may fall outside your current frame of reference:

- "Okay, your explanation of these events is . . . , right? But you think I'm saying the words but not getting it?"

- "It's difficult for you to tell me this again, since I haven't responded favorably in the past? I see it is important to you and acknowledge that it is not to me. It could be that I'm dealing with a blind spot or that we're simply stuck with a difference of judgment. I'm willing to take a deep breath now and see if I can see what I might be blind to. Let me start by telling you what I understand to be the information, reasoning, and values behind your request. Interrupt and tell me where I'm not getting it."

Step 5: Process out loud your responses to new information from others, puzzling about the fit between that new information and what's going on in your mind:

- "That's news to me. I hadn't heard that before."

- "That really throws me. How did you get to that from what you were saying?"

- "That helps me a lot by . . ."

Step 6: Structure and give closure to your sense making. Explicitly draw closure to the process of getting good information in two steps: summarize where you are in the inquiry and set next steps—for example:

- "We've run out of time. I'll summarize the gap between us on how to define the problem and then set next steps."

- "I think we're in agreement here about how to explain why it happened. I'll restate what we've agreed to; then please join me in defining next steps."

- "Obviously this is a mess. I don't have to make a decision until tomorrow morning, so let's take a break. Before we do, will you try to put the mess into words? What is it we don't understand?"

- "Clearly we have a disagreement here. Let's state it, stop, and get the next steps in place, including when and how this will be decided."

Giving good information—disclosing observational data as well as inferences, asserting our search for sense, or asserting reflective assumptions, perspectives, and values—is an act of inquiry. We offer our sense making for examination and possible change before making decisions based on it.

How to Listen: Guidelines and Tips

1. *Punch line.* You need to hear to be heard.

Different Ways of Listening

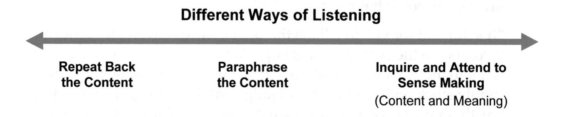

| Repeat Back the Content | Paraphrase the Content | Inquire and Attend to Sense Making (Content and Meaning) |

2. *Repeat, paraphrase, and listen for sense making.* We can use different kinds of listening depending on the circumstances. At the left end of the continuum is repeating back the actual words spoken, the literal content. In the middle of the continuum is paraphrasing the literal content of what the other person said. At the right end of the continuum is inquiry about the possible sense (or, meaning, to use a synonym) the other person might be trying to convey. We can choose to repeat back content alone, paraphrase, or attend to the person's sense making.

When listening for sense, we are not taking words literally as we do when we repeat back content. In fact, we are not paying attention to words alone, but to nuances of tone, phrasing, syntax, and demeanor. Collectively, they express the sense the person might be trying to communicate. Internally, that sense is in the form of thoughts, feelings, images, and experiences that the person is trying to form into words, which sometimes flow clearly and at other times incoherently. Our job is to accompany the person's effort to make (form) sense, not to be correcting, changing, informing, or improving on what the person appears to be saying.

3. *Choose the kind of listening that fits the context.* Here are a few examples to illustrate which type of listening might best fit different contexts or settings:

Repeating back content: Checking the facts

Receiving directions. After receiving directions for how to get from one building to another in a large complex, repeat the directions.

Doing detective work. In any kind of managerial detective work calling for reconstruction of sequences of events or what was actually said, repeat back content.

Conflict management. When serving as a third party to two or more people in conflict, repeat back content to clarify different versions of events.

Decision making. When a decision has been made, before moving on to discuss another item, restate the decision.

Paraphrasing: Distilling key points

Agenda setting. At the beginning of a staff meeting, after the leader has talked discursively about the agenda, paraphrase the major items and ask for confirmation.

Lengthy talkers. When someone has talked at length, paraphrase.

Bringing closure. When closing discussion of an agenda item, paraphrase arguments or options before restating a decision.

Meaning: Grappling with complex tasks

Supervision. When involved in almost any kind of supervisory activity where learning is the purpose, listen for meaning.

Defining a problem. When engaged in almost any kind of group effort to fathom an intractable problem or invent innovative alternatives, listen for meaning.

Offering help. When a staff member asks for help sorting out a difficult interpersonal issue, listen for meaning.

4. *Know when not to listen.* No one can or should listen all the time. Whether you listen depends in part on the nature of the information you have going into an interaction. At one extreme, the information you have can be pure speculation; at the other extreme, it can be conclusive proof, or as close to that

as possible. As a manager conducting a performance evaluation of a supervisor, if you have no information at all, you would simply be speculating about the supervisor's pattern of performance. In this case, you would need to listen and learn.

In contrast, you might know that this supervisor has a high departmental turnover rate, which leads you to speculate about the quality of the supervisor's ability to motivate and develop people. In this situation, you would have some information but not enough to be sure. Lacking confirming information, you would have to present this relationship between observable data (turnover rate) and speculative inference (not motivating and developing people?) for what it is—a speculation—and then invite the supervisor to explore the possible meanings of the observable data with you. Then structure a way for the two of you to collect data to confirm or disconfirm the possible explanations of the high turnover rate.

However, if you already had conclusive proof that you were correct, you would not be open to changing your conclusion about a pattern in a supervisor's performance. Such would be the case if your own observations were corroborated by the direct observations of three other managers, each of whom observed the same pattern of behavior in different contexts. In this case, using reflective listening might not be necessary or appropriate.

5. *Use the fill-in-the-blank method.* When trying to learn to listen for sense making, you can use this procedure:

   1. When spoken to, remember that you reflexively say to yourself, "What's the problem?" or "What do I have to do about this?"

   2. Do not get sucked into those reflexive questions. When the person stops speaking, ask yourself, as if speaking to the other person, "And that leaves you feeling . . . because of . . . ?" To fill in the first blank, you have to listen for meaning in tone. To fill in the second blank, look to the content of words.

   For example: your child says, "I don't like my teacher anymore!" You pass on the reflexive question ("What's the problem?") and call the fill-in-the-blank-question to mind: "And that leaves you feeling upset because of something your teacher did?" To make the questions sound more natural, you might then modify the phrase, and ask, "You're upset because of something your teacher did today?"

6. *Avoid errors to the extreme.* There are two predictable errors made when attempting to listen. The error to the obvious is saying back to someone who is hollering expletives, "You are angry?" The error to the shot in the dark is saying back to an employee who cannot get up in time to arrive at work on

time, "So you had problems with your mother when growing up?" Both forms of error are likely to occur as you learn to listen. In part, good judgment about when and how to listen result from risking errors to the extremes of being too literal or leaping too far from the data.

7. *Avoid "I hear you" phrases.* Do not say, "I hear what you're saying." In fact, when you hear this phrase in response to something you've said, you have a cue that the person may not be listening. Here are some other phrases indicating that the person is not going to listen but instead is going to use the idea of listening as a segue to present information to you:

   - "I know what you mean."

   - "I understand."

   - "I know how you feel."

   - "I've had that experience myself."

   - "I hear you, I hear you."

   - "I know what you're trying to say."

   Instead, strive to stay focused on the speaker's actual and unique experience. Do not assume you understand or can relate. Wait for the speaker to confirm that you do in fact understand.

8. *Watch for signs that you are not listening.* If you have not really heard what the other person is saying, he or she may keep repeating the same thing, retreat into silence, stop eye contact, or try to leave without resolution. Any of these behaviors provides you with strong feedback that you need to return to the steps outlined in the right-hand side of the listening chart in Table 3.1 seeking to understand the speaker's sense making.

9. *Watch for validation that you are listening.* A speaker who feels heard and understood may nod, say yes or something similar for confirmation, sigh, settle in a chair, soften his or her voice tone, become more reflective in tone, or disclose additional information.

10. *Switch back and forth from listening to structuring or giving good data.* Reflective listening is just one of many tools in your inquiry tool kit. Use it flexibly, and combine it with the other skills presented in this book, such as structuring and giving good data. Move fluidly from one tool to another according to the circumstances. For example, after listening reflectively, you may want to shift to structuring or giving good data when any of the following occurs:

    - When the person's tone has shifted from provocative to inquiring

- When the person has acknowledged being stuck, lost, or at wits' end

- When the person asks for help

- When you think the other person is unwilling to work with you, test that inference. If the person answers yes, then it is time to stop listening and lay out next steps or consequences.

- When you have restated the issue, problem, or event you're both looking at, tested explicitly the different meanings each of you made, and gotten confirmation from the other person ("Yes, I agree, that's where we are")

11. *Remind yourself that listening is a choice.* Copy Table 3.1 and tape it to your telephones, prop it up on your desk, or tuck it in your date book. Put it wherever you interact because you will always be getting information you do not want to hear.

   When you get information that seems wrong, surprises you, confuses you, or irritates or angers you, you will think and react automatically from the left side of Table 3.1—the reflexive problem-solving side. By glancing at the table, you will remind yourself that you can choose to put aside technical problem solving for a moment and inquire. You can attempt to understand the other person before you decide what the problem is and how to solve it.

12. *Listen when you get significant negative feedback about your own performance.* The feedback that is most significant to your learning will make no sense to you because it will fall outside your current frame of reference or set of assumptions about yourself, others, and the world. You will experience it as an attack and consider it dead wrong. You will feel the urge to refute or a surge of self-doubt. Listening under these conditions is exceptionally difficult yet of utmost importance to our learning about blind spots.

   To make matters worse, you must predict that people who need significant feedback (often us) by definition cannot get it. Significant feedback is almost always about blind spots, so others know (or think they know) that there is no way we will be open to the feedback. Consider these two examples: others do not tell someone who cannot listen that that someone cannot listen; others do not tell someone whom they fear that that someone generates fear.

   So, paradoxically, significant negative feedback about our performance is precious yet feels unnerving. Our only hope for creating conditions where others might risk giving this difficult information is the skill of listening. We assert by will our intent to be open even as our emotions are going on a wildcat strike. Then we must assert our sense making as described in "Assert

Your Search for New Sense by Using a Sequence of Steps," and "How to Give Good Information: Guidelines and Tips" in this chapter.

How to Use the Skills Together

There are only two starting points for an interaction: you are initiating the giving of information or are responding to someone else's initiative. In each situation, you need to use all three skills together, with flexibility as to sequence and emphasis. Two suggested models follow, one for each starting point:

- A model for initiating: Giving information

- A model for responding: Receiving information

These models are only as good as the improvisation that accompanies them. Every interaction is different and requires modifications in the model to take the other person into account.

A Model for Initiating: Giving Information

1. Structure

    Rationale: It takes good structure to create the conditions for good talk and listening.

    Criteria (known by both parties):
    - Background information
    - Real purpose
    - Procedure
    - Time period and place
    - Hoped-for outcome

2. Give good information

    Rationale: You have to give good data to get good data.

    Formula:
    When _____
    I feel _____
    Because _____

Guidelines:

- Give the observable data along with inferences, conclusions, and judgments.

- Give sense making, not just the results of that effort

3. Listen

Rationale: You have to hear to be heard.

Criteria:

- Tests information rather than gives

- Tests meaning rather than problem-solves

- Stays close to the data

- Is an inquiry (or a test) of possible meaning

- Is usually short

- Comes to a full stop

4. State assumed agreement or differences in data and meanings; create a structure to do joint inquiry or problem solving.

Rationale: Both parties need to be knowledgeable and in control of the agenda.

Criteria:

- A set of problem-solving steps (or inquiry, or action steps) in a sequence, each step of which answers the question, "Who does what, with whom, and when?"

- A structure can be built by both parties on the initiative of the person who called the meeting and then revised if it does not work.

5. Summarize and check for agreement.

6. Structure to close. For criteria, see step 4. To see this model in dialogue story form, read the reflective version of the "Are You Calling Me a Liar?" story.

A Model for Responding: Receiving Information

1. Listen, often more than once.
   Criteria: See step 3 in "A Model for Initiating."

2. Structure to inquire or problem-solve.
   Rationale, criteria: See step 4 in "A Model for Initiating."

3. Give good information.
   Rationale, formula, guidelines: See step 2 in "A Model for Initiating."

4. Listen.
   Criteria: See step 3 in "A Model for Initiating."

5. Structure to close.
   Criteria: See step 4 in "A Model for Initiating."

To see this model in dialogue story form, read the story "Your Spanish Is Getting Worse!" in Chapter One.

Frequently Asked Questions and Answers on Learning the Skills

Question 1: Are you saying that I am supposed to behave reflectively all of the time?
Answer: No. You couldn't even if you wanted to.

Question 2: Won't this slow down communication?
Answer: Yes, on the whole, and particularly at first, when you are learning to think and behave differently. However, reflective communication holds the promise of taking less time, not more, by breaking the competition-for-listening pattern of "they keep coming back with the same problems" (see the story by that name). People keep coming back and taking our time because we reflexively fix before we engage in interpersonal learning that leads to a better definition of what the problem actually is and how to solve it. For example, in the "Same Problems" story, the manager reflexively solves what he sees as a "lack of motivation to read the manual" problem (or a laziness problem). Through interpersonal inquiry, he finds that instead he is facing a "fear and lack of knowledge" problem. As a result, he is able to devise a solution that holds more hope of success of breaking the pattern that consumes his time: people repeatedly coming to him to solve the same problems.

Question 3: But the world moves fast! Who has the time to learn all this?
Answer: We have no urge to support us in slowing down to learn to interact differently. Our urge is to get more things done faster because our lives are packed with multiple and competing priorities at home and work. Even if we are intrigued by a lead character's performance in this book and wish we might find the same resourcefulness within ourselves, our wish to slow down is but a breeze

wafting against the gale of our urge to get more done faster. In the end, reflective thinking and behavior takes time to:

- Learn (lots of time up front is required)

- Plan (sitting before a difficult conversation to analyze our information and clarify our real purpose and procedure)

- Do (taking the other person into account as someone whose sense making will differ from ours)

We do not make a choice to take "too much time" until "taking too little time" fails us repeatedly. Speed kills, but it is also exciting and sometimes effective in getting lots of things done fast, so it is hard to give up. Learning how to think and behave reflectively becomes attractive when "too much time" is better than the alternative.

It is easy to say, although difficult to prove, that reflective skills save time in the long run. Perhaps it is fairer to say that is the hope: save time by doing it right the first time, working with other people from the outset (reflective) rather than on them (reflexive). People who feel we have worked on them revisit us later with the same problems. People who feel we are partners will work with us to find and implement solutions.

Question 4: Isn't what you propose wooden and formulaic? I like to think of myself as a unique individual and find the idea of sameness in style repelling.
Answer: The skills are presented as forms, and as such, they have the downside of being wooden and formulaic. Their upside is the structure they provide to guide us from one frame of reference to another. Getting from one frame of reference to another is frightening and can be wrenching, so the skills are structural, like bridges that make crossing possible. Of course, there is no simple crossing from one side to the other. We go back and forth constantly, the way an explorer of new territory returns home before going out again. However formulaic, the skill forms enable us to travel into new territory again, where we seek to build our tolerance and capacity for staying there. As we do, we transform these skill forms into unique expressions of our personal style. They become us rather than techniques, methods, tips, moves, or behaviors.

Question 5: Are you saying that it is rarely effective to speak emotionally? That fights are counterproductive?
Answer: No. Fights can be productive if they contribute to learning rather than entrenchment over time. And they can.

Question 6: I'm moved by the stories, but what do I do with my feelings? I want to strangle these people! That jerk of a squad leader [in "Who Said I Go Overboard?"] and the plant manager [in "Your Spanish Is Getting Worse!"]! What do the lead characters do with their feelings?!

Answer: We must learn to take care of our feelings from a reflective perspective, the way we would embrace, not scold, a child who has tripped on the sidewalk, fallen, and bloodied a knee. In effect, we would view the child's pain as legitimate because it exists, and we would trust that it would pass in the natural course of holding the child.[4] Reflectively, we embrace our feelings as a painful expression (in this example) of our courage to care and risk engagement. If we can have or accept our feelings as legitimate, then and only then can we make choices about whether and how to give them expression, while inquiring into the circumstances that produced them. In contrast, our current relationship to our feelings is not reflective but reflexive, as in "What's wrong? Fix it." We start from the assumption that something is wrong when we are in pain and automatically:

- Attribute conscious negative intent to the person who did something that triggered our pain

- Attempt to fix ourselves by ridding ourselves of the feelings of pain because they are evidence of being wrong or failure: we suppress or repress or speak judgmentally or blamefully

Because by definition we have been wronged and have the pain to prove it, our sense of responsibility and integrity is invested in setting right the people who wronged us: the squad leaders and plant managers of the world.

Question 7: You seem to be saying that two people can look at the same event and see it differently and neither person is necessarily wrong. Are you saying there are no qualitative differences in perception?

Answer: No. There are qualitative differences in perception.

Question 8: Are you saying that fix-it communication is wrong? That we shouldn't do it?

Answer: No. Reflexive fixing applied to people is not wrong, only limited.

Question 9: Can you be saying that there is something wrong with criticism and reassurance?

Answer. Wrong, no. Limited, yes, particularly if you are blind to the fact that you are stuck in only these two forms of behavior. You want criticism and reassurance to be part of a broader and more flexible interpersonal repertoire.

Question 10: Are you suggesting that the only filters and frames for making reflective sense of the world are those given in this book?
Answer. No.

Action: Questions and Answers on Using and Valuing Reflective Skills

This book asks you to hold questions of application aside until you have learned to produce the skills through practice. The bet is that producing the skills (even in protected settings and low-risk relationships) will change the nature of your perception of application problems and enable you to find ways to use the skills that you would never have imagined when you lacked skill. Still, there are questions about application that, if answered, can free people to invest in practice and action. Typical questions and answers to them follow below.

First, though, a word about the most predictable application problem. Taking reflective action often requires that we interact with a fault-finding, fix-it frame of reference without switching to our own fix-it mode in the process. You can reread "The Cord of Wood," the second version of "Are You Calling Me a Liar?" and "They Come Back with the Same Problems" to analyze the lead characters' attempts to take into account people who are coming at them from a fix-it frame of reference. Ask yourself what you can learn about this difficult problem by studying the characters' thinking and behavior in these three stories.

In the "Who Said I Go Overboard?" story, there is no internal dialogue to learn from explicitly, but it is a remarkable confrontation between the talk-tough and talk-sense approaches to communication. Reread it asking yourself how Mike might be thinking about what he is doing to create conditions for interpersonal inquiry instead of reverting to fix-it manipulation. For a more rigorous exercise, at every point where you would have turned fix-it on Wayne, write down what you would really like to say to him. With Mike's reflective response juxtaposed with your reflexive response, draw on the knowledge you have gained by reading this book to write rational statements to explain why Mike was more disciplined than you. Surely these will only be hypotheses, but the exercise will force you to articulate and organize your own version of reflective assumptions, perspectives, and practices.

Question 1: Aren't you closing your eyes to how the world actually works? If you go out there and listen, you'll get your head handed to you!
Answer: At worst, much of the interpersonal world is hostile to reflective practice. So be discriminating about where, when, and with whom you try to behave reflectively. Do not begin with predictably talk-tough types and difficult interpersonal situations. By analogy to your reading this book, were you to take a set of tennis lessons without ever having played the game before, you would not

164

call your professional friend for a game (unless you wanted to experience the shame of having your new skills desert you the moment the pro hits you a 100-mile-an-hour serve). The claim here is that if you risk practicing to a moderate level of proficiency before you take your new skill into the real world, then take action first with people you trust and interact with regularly, you will begin to perceive and make opportunities for success in the real world, where the challenges for successful implementation are greater.

Question 2: Where are we supposed to begin without getting chewed up?
Answer: Discipline yourself to practice first with your children and second with trusted adults in your home and work life. Then try to use the skills in relatively benign situations at work where other people are clearly seeking your help in thinking something through.

Question 3: You can't force someone to search for sense with you, right? What do you do if they won't and they have to change?
Answer: In the end, you cannot force someone to join you in reflecting on their own practice to learn and change. That's a central premise of reflective practice: learning is a choice. It cannot be mandated. However, let's assume that you hold a position of leadership in an organization (or a family, though the language to follow will not be appropriate to families), and someone who reports to you "has to change." In this circumstance, you must combine the use of personal power (what this book is about) and positional power compassionately, judiciously, and firmly. Positional power is expressed in part in the form of a peashooter-to-bazooka continuum of organizational consequences.[5] The continuum varies from position to position, organization to organization, and culture to culture. If acting through your peashooter-to-bazooka continuum does not work and you cannot get rid of the person, you figure out how to live with the situation by containing it or minimizing its consequences to others and the organization or family.

Question 4: But the people who most need to look at themselves won't. That's the point. So, how do these skills help me with those people?
Answer: Though limited, your chances of success are often much better with reflective learning skills than reflexive fix-it skills. In both the "Are You Calling Me a Liar?" and "Who Said I Go Overboard?" stories, you have people who fit the category of most in need of looking at themselves but won't. The first version of both stories shows a flaw-finding, fix-it approach, and the results in "Liar" are a lawyer at the next meeting and, in "Overboard," a shouting match. The second version of each story shows a reflective approach, and in "Liar" the "bad guy," Mitch, actually begins to reflect on and take responsibility for his thinking and behavior. This is a hopeful (though far from conclusive) result. Still, the result is extraordinary when compared to a lawyer coming to the next meeting. In "Overboard," Mike fails to engage Wayne in examining his own practice, so he

clearly failed to get the result he sought. And yet he did get another result: he built the relationship. Understanding, trust, and respect were a result.

From a reflective perspective, we are trying to achieve two simultaneous results in every interaction: improved performance or product and an enhanced relationship characterized by trust and respect. Communication as interpersonal learning is the way to get there. Over the long haul, achieving one result without the other is problematic in organizations and families.

Question 5: In the meetings I attend, people are out to nail you and take advantage of any weakness. You think these skills will work there?

Answer: If you are right about these people's motivation, probably not. If you have great judgment about which skill to use when and a masterful repertoire, then perhaps. But don't start in meetings. Use the skills in one-on-one contact with meeting participants, beginning with the person you trust most.

Question 6: This touchy-feely stuff hasn't worked for me before. Why should your version work any better?

Answer: Typically people using similar skills neither understand nor believe in them as other than new manipulative gimmicks. That is, their intention is to expand their reflexive repertoire, not question and change it. As a result, the skills often come off as a set of manipulative gimmicks or techniques, which they are when used in that way. Other people attribute the "new bag of tricks" to "charm school" and respond in kind. As a result, the newly "skilled" person concludes, "This touchy-feely stuff will never work." Again, typically, other efforts fail because the level of skill is mismatched with the forces at work in the situation. Out of desperation or impatience or false hope, many people try out learning skills in the real world long before they can produce them in protected settings where risk is low. In the real world where risk is high, the chances for success are minimal.

Question 7: Am I supposed to get as inner as the characters in these stories?

Answer: The stories are more inner than most of us can or would want to be. Think of the stories not as representations of real life but as real life being studied in a seminar, and imagine the stories as life in self-conscious slow motion. We often watch performances on videotape in slow motion to better observe what is actually happening. That is the hope here, where the stories split their focus between the observable dialogue and the inner sense making of the lead characters.

Often there is an excessive innerness that accompanies personal growth during the phases of discovery and invention because those phases are about changing our internal dialogue. During this period of our learning, many of us struggle with a fear that is voiced as paralysis of analysis. We must respect this fear, even as we decline its call to stop questioning.

It is difficult to question the reflexive frame of reference that is our truth or, put differently, the very ground we stand on. Without questioning, there is no discovery. Still, the result is painful: we no longer can think and act confidently from the frame of reference that was our unquestioned truth, but we have not yet constructed a new reflective voice we can trust. During this transition period, we fear that our questioning might bring us to a paralytic stop in self-conscious darkness when we hoped it would initiate the start of a brilliant journey. Through repeated practice and action, we become less labored in our new self-consciousness and more fluid in inventing new, reflective thinking and behavior.

Nevertheless, by definition, being reflective requires more self-consciousness than we are used to when living in a reflexive internal world.

Question 8: What do you have to say about doing this with bosses?

Answer: Proceed cautiously unless there is high trust between you and your boss and your boss has asked explicitly for a two-way exchange of performance information.

Difficult relationships with bosses often present a question that applies to using the skills with anyone: How can we give feedback to people who are (or might be) blind to the behavior we want to discuss? Specifically, for example, can we talk to bosses about their failure to listen? Almost all bosses advocate some form of open communication, whether it is an open-door policy or they say they are open to feedback. Yet we have seen our bosses behave otherwise (or appear to). Do we dare talk to our bosses about such a discrepancy, particularly when talking to a colleague or subordinate is itself a high-risk endeavor? Most of us fail at this kind of communication much more than we succeed. So trying to do it with a boss usually poses too large a risk.

Question 9: Don't you think you're setting us up for failure here? These stories are too neat and life is messy.

Answer: Taken as a group, the stories can come off as too neat or too pat, or as having too many happy endings. So collectively, the stories risk promising an overly simple view of the personal and interpersonal world. That is the opposite of their intent, which is to communicate that the interpersonal world is not simple but complex. This limitation in the form of the stories should be weighed against the vitality of the vision they present of significantly different possibilities for human interaction.

Question 10: Are you saying that there is something wrong with the exercise of power and authority? That's nuts!

Answer: No. That would indeed be nuts.

Question 11: Are you saying that the exercise of power and authority inhibit learning and have a negative impact on others? Ridiculous!

Answer: No. Such a conclusion would certainly be ridiculous.

Question 12: Reflective skills aren't a substitute for exercising positional power. Right?

Answer: Right! This book focuses on making decisions about giving and receiving information as an act of interpersonal learning. It makes a case for why we should decide to disclose information rather than withhold, listen rather than criticize or reassure, and structure for interpersonal learning rather than unilateral control. In effect, if we hold a certain position, these decisions in favor of reflective practice are decisions about how to go about doing what our position requires.

Chapter Six

Conceptual Summary

When we communicate with others, we instinctively rely on a core part of ourselves, here called a reflexive frame of reference. Although our reflexive selves function well in technical settings where fault finding and fixing things are appropriate to the content, that same frame of reference has two major limitations when applied in the world of interpersonal relationships:

1. It conducts our relations with others through closed agendas, withholding of data, and criticism or reassurance, with the result of engendering mistrust, the most corrosive ingredient in human affairs.

2. It insists on taking the sense in our heads and stuffing it into the heads of others, teaching others to trust our sense more than their own, and forfeiting opportunities to develop proficiency and trust in joint sense making.

This book begins with a story that portrays our entrapment within the limitations of our reflexive frame of reference. The family relationships in "A Son Drops Out of College" are characterized by a lack of trust and an inability to join in making new sense together. Though they love their son, the parents cannot engage in sense making with him. Instead, they attempt to fix him by telling him tacitly to abandon his own sense and substitute theirs.

The contrasting consequences of repeating this reflexive pattern, on the one hand, or of breaking it, on the other, can be imagined by picturing Ben, the son in the story, as the lead character in two later stories: first in "Triumph at Work, Trouble at Home," and then in "Who Says I Go Overboard?"

If the family in the "Son" story reverts to reflexive form and continues fixing one another, then we can picture Ben twenty-five years later as the CEO in the "Triumph" story, incapable of making sense of his home life and unaware that the trouble at home also awaits him at work. Why would he be able to join with his wife or colleagues at work in making new sense of his own behavior if all he had ever experienced was being fixed? Wouldn't he simply be a fixer too?

By contrast, if the family in the "Son" story breaks the fix-it pattern of their interaction and develops the capacity to talk sense, we can imagine Ben growing up to be like Mike in the "Overboard" story. In this scenario, he is not a fixer. He talks sense, and he communicates to lead and learn. And why not? Having experienced the mutual trust and effectiveness fostered by his parents' practice of reflective behavior, why wouldn't he extend the same opportunity to others?

As he develops his own reflective skills through the learning cycle of discovery, invention, practice, and action, why wouldn't he invite others to join him on that journey?

For those who accept the invitation, the following conceptual summary may be useful in reorienting themselves when they inevitably become lost or confused on the path to reflective practice.

Where We Start From: A Reflexive Frame of Reference

1. The conditions of the distant past under which humans evolved required quick, defensive, fight-or-flight reflexes for survival.

2. Culturally, the present and future conditions in our culture are quite different, characterized by constant change, interdependence, complexity, and diversity. But our basic reflexes have not changed.

3. Interpersonally, these reflexes perpetuate a competition-for-listening pattern of interaction in which we are constantly frustrated in our requests to be listened to while frustrating others by not listening.

4. The result of these cultural and interpersonal conditions is that we continually experience moments of anxiety and uncertainty about how to make sense of and respond to events.

5. Our reflexes are not capable of responding effectively because they evolved to cope with a different set of conditions.

6. Based on an either-or right-wrong assumption, our reflexes cause us to experience people who present information that is different ("not right," in our terms) as wrong.

7. Starting from this assumption, we feel threatened and think we must act to fix what's at fault.

8. Our feelings and thoughts lead to reflexive behavior, in which we:

    • Operate with closed agendas, structuring interactions for control.

    • Withhold observed data and the process of searching for sense.

    • Criticize or reassure rather than listen.

9. In a reflexive mode, our assumptions, thinking, and behavior are automatic and experienced as fixed, not flexible.

10. To communicate effectively, we need new reflective skills better adapted to current and future conditions of change and uncertainty, which require us to continuously make new sense and invent new ways of behaving.

Two Frames of Reference

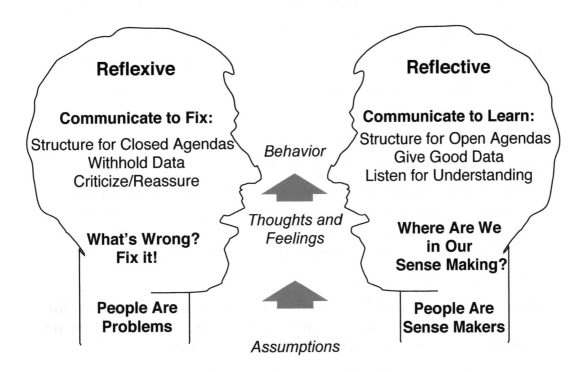

Where We Are Headed: A Reflective Frame of Reference

1. Human evolution has given us the capability to reflect and act in ways other than purely by reflex.

2. Our current and future conditions are characterized by constant change, interdependence, complexity, and diversity, requiring us to reflect, learn, and invent new behavior continually.

3. As we do this, we frequently experience moments of anxiety and uncertainty about how to make sense of and respond to events.

4. Despite anxiety and uncertainty, we can choose to engage in ongoing inquiry into our sense making and behavior. Both are open to change in response to the new data generated by inquiry.

5. How we make sense and behave are choices.

6. Interpersonally, we can choose to break the competition-for-listening pattern of interaction.

7. We can adopt and develop the assumption that people (including ourselves) are sense makers, so that we do not view every interaction as though it has to be either-or or right or wrong, but view it as a matter of legitimate differences in sense making that cannot be explained by using either-or assumptions.

8. This new assumption allows us to feel less threatened by differences, and we can think about where we and the other person are in our sense making.

9. New feeling and thinking can lead to reflective behavior, in which we

   • Operate with open agendas, structuring interactions to share control

   • Disclose observed data and our process of searching for sense

   • Listen for understanding

10. In a reflective mode, our assumptions, thinking, and behavior are experienced as flexible, not automatic or fixed.

11. We can continue to develop these new skills of reflective communication, which are better adapted to current and future conditions of change and uncertainty, enabling us to continuously make new sense and invent new ways of behaving. The result is that learning becomes integral to action.

12. The phases of growth to this result are:

   Discovery: Getting located. We must discover and accept responsibility for the gaps between our ideal and actual communication, to gain insight into the reflexive fault-finding frame of reference that causes them.

   Invention: Choosing a guide. We must invent and learn to trust a reflective sense-making voice that can listen to and question our reflexive interpretations of our internal and interpersonal experience, then assert alternative ways of making sense and behaving.

   Practice: Getting prepared (in a protected setting). We must practice how to embody in our behavior the values of open agendas, disclosure, and listening and then evaluate and adjust our new behavior with the guidance of a reflective voice (our own or a partner's).

   Action: Walking the talk (in the real world). We must act to move our communication from a fault-finding (reflexive) frame of reference to a sense-making (reflective) one, and renew this intention through a continuous cycle of discovery, invention, practice, and action.

Talking Sense: A Process Map

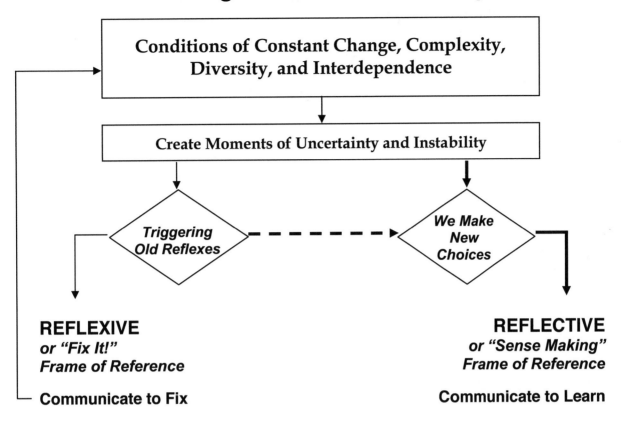

Conditions of Constant Change, Complexity, Diversity, and Interdependence

Create Moments of Uncertainty and Instability

Triggering Old Reflexes

We Make New Choices

REFLEXIVE
or "Fix It!"
Frame of Reference

Communicate to Fix

REFLECTIVE
or "Sense Making"
Frame of Reference

Communicate to Learn

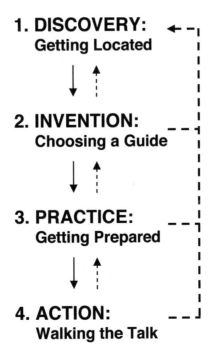

1. DISCOVERY:
Getting Located

2. INVENTION:
Choosing a Guide

3. PRACTICE:
Getting Prepared

4. ACTION:
Walking the Talk

Talking Sense: A Process Map

Notes

Chapter One

1. Leticia Peña, currently professor of management at the University of Wisconsin–La Crosse, wrote the first draft of this story and contributed to later drafts.

2. John Northrop, currently the executive director of the Alabama School of Fine Arts, wrote the framework for both versions of this story, the substance of the reflexive version here, and the first draft of the reflective version in Chapter Three.

Chapter Two

1. I first heard this distinction made by Kiyo Morimoto.

2. A generalized version of this exercise can be found in the "Discovery" section of Chapter Five.

3. D. H. Lawrence, *Studies in Classic American Literature* (London: Penguin, 1924, p. 57).

Chapter Three

1. John Northrop, currently the executive director of the Alabama School of Fine Arts, wrote the framework for both versions of this story, the substance of the reflexive version here, and the first draft of the reflective version in Chapter One.

2. The lines of dialogue in this longer story are numbered, as are those of some of the other stories to follow. These stories are recommended for study during the practice and action phases of your learning, and the numbering provides for easy reference.

3. The boundary conditions that are necessary to create conditions for interpersonal learning are not confined to clear and shared purpose, procedure, and time period, though these are the conditions focused on here. For example, boundary conditions are set by saying no (you can't have the car tonight; you can't take tomorrow as a personal day). On the surface of it, saying no appears to preclude rather than produce conditions for inquiry. Surely, this can be true and should be sometimes. At the same time, saying no can open joint inquiry: without proper limits, some people are unable or unwilling to engage in interpersonal learning. For example, setting boundary conditions (in the form of invoking sanctions that range from a verbal reprimand, to a written reprimand, to withholding a bonus) regarding unacceptable behavior at home or work can be necessary to create conditions for interpersonal learning. As long as people

are allowed to behave out of bounds without sanction, why would they engage in exploring the issues involved in an attempt to change the pattern?

4. A "Yes, But" section defines typical concerns and quandaries we often experience when contemplating the use of the particular skill.

5. Robert Bolton, *People Skills* (New York: Simon & Schuster, 1986).

6. The table is not meant to imply a one-to-one correspondence between the questions on the left and right, nor is it meant to imply that we ask (or should ask) the questions on either side in the sequence listed, or that we ask (or should ask) all of the questions each time we receive information.

7. You must believe this voice to act on it, and before you believe it you must have grown in the sense of legitimizing your own internal experience. To develop our reflective voice, we have to challenge our reflexive assumption that feelings, yearnings, and conditions of searching for sense or no sense are illegitimate rather than legitimate parts of ourselves. Experienced as illegitimate, as toxic deficiencies, they must either be gotten rid of (blown off, vented, acted out, expressed, excised) or eaten (suppressed, repressed, sat on, hidden, denied) before we can be worthy individuals or competent professionals. The reflective alternative to exploding or imploding these experiences is to be with them, to have them, to accept them as resources for our learning rather than as liabilities. We cannot learn about or from something we do not have.

Chapter Four

1. In the following articles, Jentz and Murphy argue that confusion is an increasingly inescapable part of leaders' lives and must be used as a resource for personal and organizational improvement:

- Barry C. Jentz and Jerome T. Murphy, "Embracing Confusion: What Leaders Do When They Don't Know What to Do," *Phi Delta Kappan, 86*(5), January 2005, pp. 358–366.
- Barry C. Jentz and Jerome T. Murphy, "Starting Confused: How Leaders Start When They Don't Know Where to Start," *Phi Delta Kappan, 86*(10), June 2005, pp. 736–744.

2. Two of the stories have two versions: the normal reflexive handling and the contrasting reflective mode advocated here. In one, the way advocated here actually occurred in real life, and I constructed the contrasting normal dialogue. In the other, the normal dialogue actually occurred, and I wrote the new dialogue as an expression of how the exchange might have gone had the writer used the reflective skills recommended here. The stories are formatted differently so readers can find different ways to connect with the characters and the ideas offered through their experience. Any names used in the stories are fictitious.

3. He does not yet have the data-giving skill of asserting his sense making along the way during the interaction, but his private sense making demonstrates the skill of discovery and evidences prior invention of a reflective voice that is developed enough to guide him in producing a listening response, albeit literal at the outset. As he makes his way through a paraphrase of the client's literal content, he sees through to the sense that is tacit in the content, lack of trust, and inquires about that insight in the form of listening for understanding.

4. Chris Gearin, currently the president of Hickey College in St. Louis, wrote the framework for the contrasting stories here, the substance of the reflexive story, and the first draft of the reflective story. He took part in editing revised drafts of the reflective story.

Chapter Five

1. I first heard this idea from Kiyo Morimoto.
2. I first heard this distinction made by Kiyo Morimoto.
3. I first heard this idea from Kiyo Morimoto.
4. I first heard this analogy used by Kiyo Morimoto.
5. Each position in an organization has a peashooter-to-bazooka continuum of consequences to bring out-of-bounds behavior in bounds. Here is a continuum of incremental steps between the extremes of ignoring an out-of-bounds behavior and firing a person because of that behavior:

- Verbal inquiry about the out-of-bounds behavior, offer of help if appropriate
- Verbal inquiry, discussion of how to ensure that a pattern does not emerge, offer of help if appropriate
- Verbal inquiry about the pattern of behavior, help offered in the form of jointly developing an action plan for stopping the behavior, with notification that a next event will be written and placed in the person's file
- Written reprimand, with a notification that a history of prior events will be written in an overview memo and placed in the person's file
- Written overview placed in the file, with notification of how other managers will be involved if the out-of-bounds behavior continues
- Written poor performance evaluation
- Transfer

Further Reading

- Argyris, Chris, and Schön, Donald. *Theory in Action: Increasing Professional Effectiveness*. San Francisco: Jossey-Bass, 1974.

- Bolton, Robert. *People Skills*. Upper Saddle River, N.J.: Prentice Hall, 1979.

- Covey, Stephen R. *The Seven Habits of Highly Effective People*. New York: Simon & Schuster, 1989.

- Fisher, Roger, and Ury, William. *Getting to Yes: Negotiating Agreement Without Giving In*. Boston: Houghton Mifflin, 1981.

- Kotter, John P. *Power and Influence: Beyond Formal Authority*. New York: Free Press, 1985.

- Langer, Ellen. *Mindfulness*. Reading, Mass.: Addison-Wesley, 1989.

- Lynd, Helen Merrell. *On Shame and the Search for Identity*. Hoboken, N.J.: Wiley, 1958.

- Naisbitt, John. *Megatrends*. New York: Warner Books, 1982.

- Patterson, Kerry, Grenny, Joseph, McMillan, Ron, and Switzler, Al. *Crucial Conversations*. New York: McGraw-Hill, 2002.

- Perry, William G., Jr. *Forms of Intellectual and Ethical Development*. New York: Henry Holt, 1968.

- Schön, Donald. *Beyond the Stable State*. London: Temple Smith, 1971.

- Schön, Donald. *The Reflective Practitioner: How Professionals Think in Action*. New York: Basic Books, 1983.

- Stone, Douglas, Patton, Bruce, and Heen, Sheila. *Difficult Conversations*. New York: Penguin Books, 2000.

About the Author

For more than twenty years, Barry Jentz has taught courses in leadership and communication at the Harvard Graduate School of Education, and he has authored numerous articles and four books (two published by McGraw-Hill and two by his company Leadership and Learning, Inc.) about his approach to helping leaders and organizations improve their performance. He is founder and co-owner of Leadership and Learning, Inc., an organizational consulting firm with a focus in leadership development, team building, and organizational change–whose widely diverse practice includes educational organizations (more than sixty public and private schools/systems, community colleges, colleges, graduate schools of education), nonprofits, professional firms, and businesses (as diverse as newspaper publishing, finance, travel, nuclear power, marketing, construction, real estate development, and international management consulting). During thirty-seven years of practice, he has invented widely used methodologies for improving performance, including the EntryPlan approach to beginning a new job. Barry graduated from Kenyon College (B.A.) and from the Harvard Graduate School of Education (M.A.T.). He began his career as a high school teacher and trained as an organizational consultant at the National Training Laboratories (NTL); he created and led of one of the first public alternative high schools in the country, the Murray Road School in Newton, Mass.; and he was a founding member of the Leadership and Learning Collaborative (LLC), a Carnegie Foundation–funded effort to invent new forms of professional development for administrators in public school systems, which was a precursor of principal centers around the country.

About Leadership and Learning, Inc.

Since 1975, Barry Jentz and Joan Wofford have been partners and principals in Leadership and Learning, Inc., an organizational development and consulting firm specializing in leadership development, organizational change, and team building. Between us, we have over seventy years of consulting experience, working extensively in both the public and private sectors with administrators, managers, and executives in public school systems, independent schools, higher education and education-related agencies, government and social service agencies, and day care facilities. Our experience includes businesses as diverse as newspaper publishing, finance, nuclear power, architectural design and construction, real estate development, international management consulting, engineering, consumer products, software development, and magazine publishing, along with associations of doctors, lawyers, and architects.

Our business is making learning an integral part of leadership: We believe that leaders must be capable of learning about and modifying their own practice by examining the underlying patterns of thought that give rise to that practice, as well as generate this same capability in those who work for them. Our methodologies engage leaders in examining and changing their own behavior and underlying mental constructions by:

- Creating new personal and interpersonal knowledge through the Myers-Briggs Type Indicator
- Helping individual leaders make new sense of their experience and increase their vocabulary of leadership behavior through executive coaching
- Construing the start of a new job as an opportunity for organizational learning by using an entry plan approach
- Producing change in individual and teamwork performance through a progression of group teamwork performance feedback activities
- Expanding interpersonal skills through videotaping and analysis of a progression of difficult managerial interactions
- Enhancing the performance of large teams through an off-site, all-on-the-same-page, problem-solving activity and other designs to help groups identify, examine, change, and improve their own work structures and processes

Index

Y

SKILLFUL TEACHING

The Skillful Teacher: The Comprehensive Resource for Improving Teaching and Learning (7th ed. 2018)
Updates the last edition with powerful new material and 100+ videos illustrating the skills. Designed for both the novice and the experienced educator, *The Skillful Teacher* is a unique synthesis of the Knowledge Base on Teaching, with repertoires for matching teaching strategies to student needs. Designed as a practical guide for practitioners working to broaden their teaching skills, the book combines theory with practice and focuses on 18 critical areas of classroom performance. A must for instructional coaches and mentors.
by Jon Saphier, Mary Ann Haley-Speca, & Robert Gower

High Expectations Teaching: How to Persuade Students to Believe and Act on "Smart Is Something You Can Get"
(2017)
For all the productive conversation around "mindsets," what's missing are the details of how to convince our discouraged and underperforming students that "smart is something you can get." Until now. With the publication of *High-Expectations Teaching*, Jon Saphier reveals once and for all evidence that the bell curve of ability is plain wrong—that ability is something that can be grown significantly if we can first help students to believe in themselves.
by Jon Saphier

Activators: Activity Structures to Engage Students' Thinking Before Instruction (1993)
This book is a collection of classroom-tested, practical activity structures for getting students' minds active and engaged prior to introducing new content or skills.
by Jon Saphier & Mary Ann Haley

Summarizers: Activity Structures to Support Integration and Retention of New Learning (1993)
This book is a collection of classroom-tested, practical activity structures for getting students cognitively active during and after periods of instruction.
by Jon Saphier & Mary Ann Haley

SKILLFUL LEADERSHIP

Transforming Ineffective Teams: Maximizing Collaboration's Impact on Learning: The Skillful Leader II (2008)
This important "Skillful Leader" book arms administrators and teacher leaders with step-by-step strategies to confront and raise the performance of teams and individuals who undermine student learning. The text includes methods of collecting data, strategies for intervention, and tips for hiring and training. Individual and community profiles, together with legal notes, provide practical tools for busy leaders.
by Alexander D. Platt, Caroline E. Tripp, Robert G. Fraser, James R. Warnock, & Rachel E. Curtis

Strengthening Teacher Evaluation: Taking Action to Improve Ineffective Teaching (The Skillful Leader III) (2014)
This work serves as a how-to handbook to accompany the best selling *The Skillful Leader: Confronting Mediocre Teaching*. Like its predecessor, the book offers dozens of illustrations, new cases, and sample documents plus legal advice to help evaluators confront ineffective instruction. It is a cover-to-cover guide for solving thorny teacher performance problems.
by Alexander D. Platt & Caroline E. Tripp

Beyond Mentoring: Putting Instructional Focus on Comprehensive Induction Programs (2011)
This book emphasizes the critical role of instructional practice in the induction support that is given to new and beginning teachers. Using RBT's model for the comprehensive induction of new teachers, educators are guided through the steps of developing an induction plan for new teachers and integrating the induction program with the district's professional learning community.
by Jon Saphier, Susan Freedman, & Barbara Aschheim

Talk Sense: Communicating to Lead and Learn (2007)
Barry Jentz shows how leaders can build the requisite trust and credibility for improving organizational performance. Typically, leaders "talk tough" to improve performance. When that doesn't work, they "talk nice" (or vice-versa). By learning to "talk sense", leaders can succeed in their efforts to improve performance.
by Barry Jentz

Research for Better Teaching, Inc. • One Acton Place, Acton, MA 01720 USA • Phone +1 978-263-9449
Web: www.RBTeach.com • Email: pubs@RBTeach.com

SKILLFUL DATA USE

The Data Coach's Guide to Improving Learning for All Students: Unleashing the Power of Collaborative Inquiry (2008)

This resource helps Data-Team facilitators move schools away from unproductive data practices and toward examining data for systematic and continuous improvement in instruction and learning. The book includes a CD-ROM with slides and reproducibles.
by Nancy Love, Katherine E. Stiles, Susan Mundry, & Kathryn DiRanna

Laminated Guide: ***Data Literacy for Teachers*** (2011)

For every teacher, Data Coach, and inquiry team. In a fold-out 8.5" x 11" laminated form, ready to be inserted in a notebook, the guide provides a simple framework to help teachers feel comfortable, knowledgeable, and skilled in effectively using a variety of data, including formative assessments.
by Nancy Love

Laminated Guide: ***The Skillful Inquiry/Data Team*** (2012)

For every grade level (elementary) or subject-area (middle and high school) team of teachers, plus school and district administrators. In a fold-out 8.5" x 11" laminated form, ready to be inserted in a notebook, this guide provides a proven-effective inquiry process and practical tools to maximize their impact on student achievement.
by Nancy Love

DVD: ***The Skillful Data Use Series*** (2012) Volume 1 Collaborative Inquiry: Connecting Data to Results. DVD collection of introductory instructional videos based on *The Data Coach's Guide* and *Using Data to Improve Learning for All* provides expert commentary, insights from successful implementations, and views of Data Teams in action.

Posters: ***Unleashing the Power of Collaborative Inquiry*** (2009)

Eight full-color, 24" x 36" laminated posters: (1) Using Data 19 Tasks, (2) Building the Bridge, (3) Using Data Diagram, (4) Data Driven Dialogue, (5) Data Triangle, (6) Logic Model, (7) Verify Causes Tree, (8) Drill Down Deep. Data is power!

OTHER RBT RESOURCES

John Adams' Promise: How to Have Good Schools for <u>All</u> Our Children, Not Just for Some (2005)

Curriculum reform, structural reform, funding reform, organizational reform—all these 20th-century efforts have failed to make a significant dent in the achievement gap and the performance of disadvantaged students, especially in cities and poor rural areas.
by Jon Saphier

How to Bring Vision to School Improvement Through Core Outcomes, Commitments and Beliefs (1993)

This practical guide provides a proven step-by-step sequence for generating consensus among parents and staff about a few valued core outcomes they want for all children. Then it shows how to achieve the concrete outcomes in the areas of school and family life.
by Jon Saphier & John D'Auria